Wealthy Me Goldsbrough
First Edition 2020

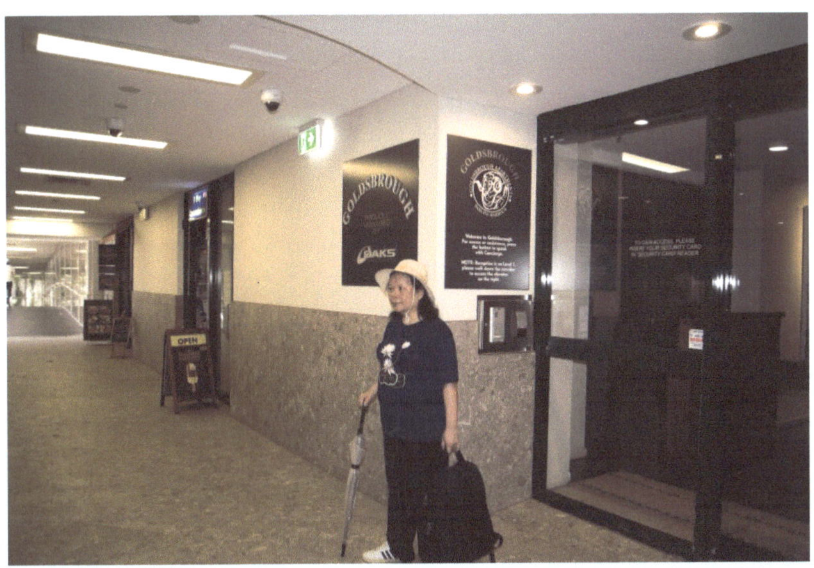

Wealthy Me Goldsbrough presents Sydney's charming Darling Harbour and the surroundings within walking distance, accompanied with a brief history of the area and inspirational quotes from Baha'i writings, the Bible, Buddha, Eastern and Western philosophers, scientists and writers. It showcases apartments hosted by Minh Hien and Farshid within an architecturally renovated historic Goldsbrough building through colourful photos and provides practical guide.

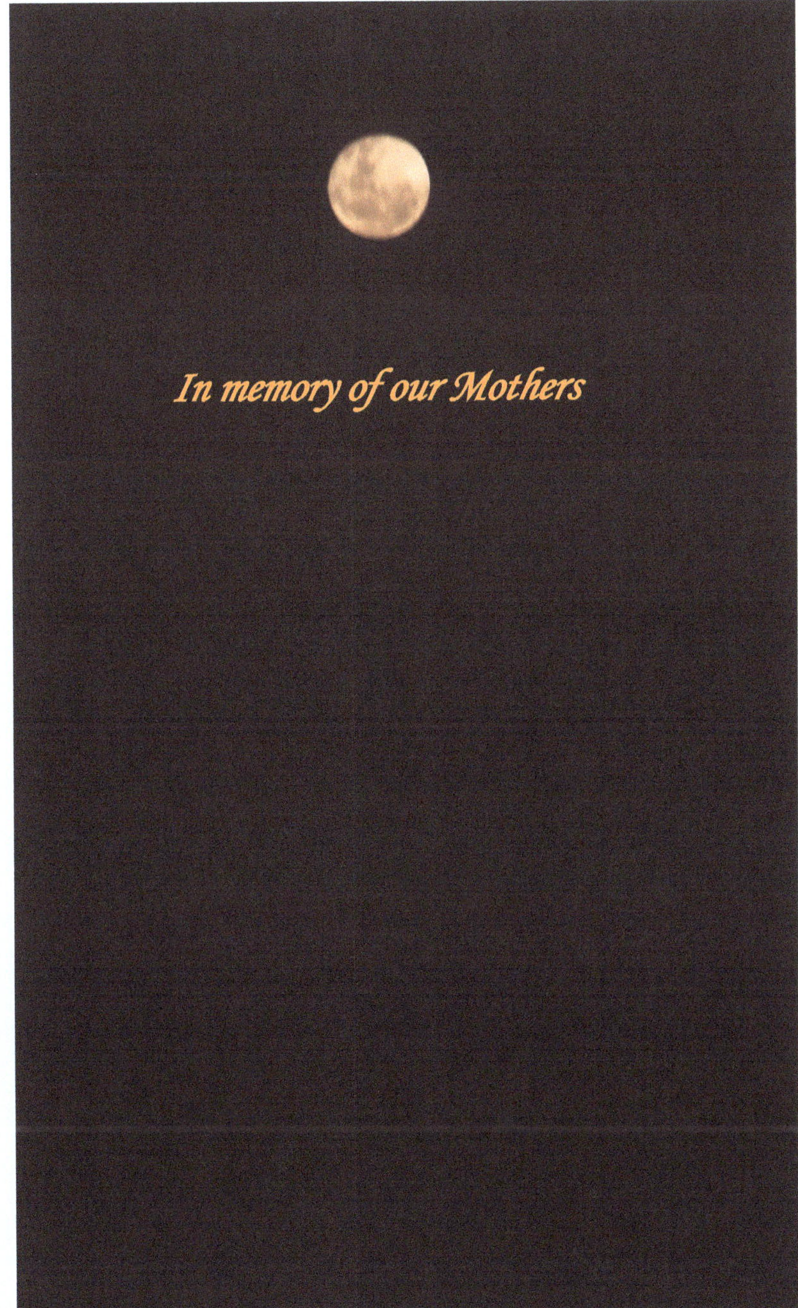
In memory of our Mothers

Published on 31 December 2020 by Minh Hien Pty Limited
ABN 86 086 458 817
www.minh-hien.com

Inquiries should be addressed to
Minh Hien Pty Limited
PO Box 737
Drummoyne NSW 1470
Australia.

This edition is released under the brand name: *Wealthy Me®*
in memory of our mothers.

Creators: Hien Minh Thi Tran and Farshid Anvari.

Title: Wealthy Me Goldsbrough.

ISBN: 9780994602862 (paperback)

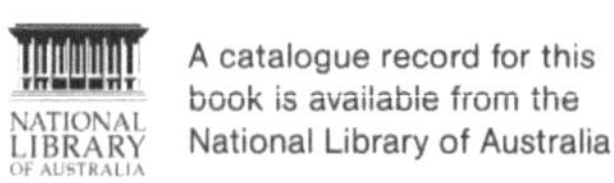

A catalogue record for this
book is available from the
National Library of Australia

‘Let your vision be world embracing
rather than confined to your own self.’
Bahá'u'lláh

About the Creators

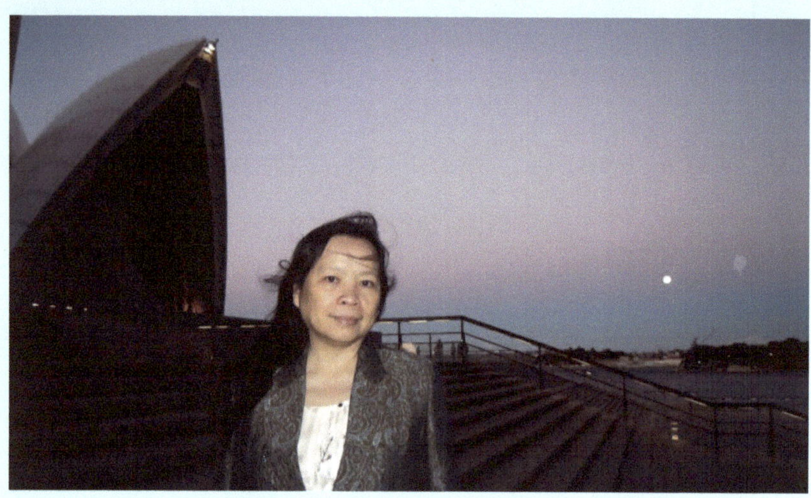

Hien Minh Thi Tran (Minh Hiền) is an author and an educational consultant. She holds qualifications in the fields of education, engineering, accounting, commerce, management and writing. She was selected to participate in the 2019 Hardcopy National Professional Development Program to write her memoir. In 2006, she was awarded the Australian Society of Authors Mentorship. She is featured in the 2008 Who's Who in Tasmania. She loves to record life experiences through writing. She speaks Vietnamese and English fluently.

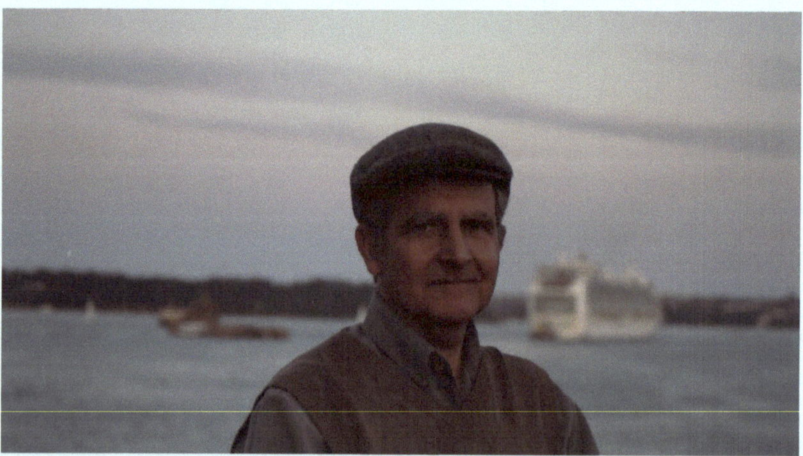

Farshid is a researcher, an engineer and an educational consultant. He was working in various industries in Melbourne, Hobart and Sydney for three decades. He loves to capture the beauty and happiness of life through photography. He speaks Persian and English fluently.

CONTENTS

Book cover photos:

Front: The main entrance of the Goldsbrough building

Back: Darling Harbour, Sydney

Photos were taken on 29 Nov 2020.

'We went through fire and through water: but thou brought us out into a wealthy place.'

Psalm 66:12.

Wealthy Me Goldsbrough

We created Wealthy Me Goldsbrough in December 2020.

The pandemic COVID-19 had a big influence in creating it.

The first known person to have contracted COVID-19 was found in late 2019. After that, COVID-19 spread rapidly throughout the World.

In March 2020, the government of Australia stopped all international travellers from entering the country.

One of the first states in Australia that introduced tougher border restriction to travellers was the island state of Tasmania. On 19 March 2020 the Tasmanian government declared a State of Emergency and closed their borders.

Soon after that other States followed.

Between March 2020 and the end of November 2020 and, again in late December 2020, most States closed their borders to people from New South Wales, NSW.

In the beginning of December 2020 when the borders began to open we started Wealthy Me Goldsbrough to host guests in our apartments in the Goldsbrough building, Darling Harbour, Sydney.

This edition was compiled during the most difficult time while Darling Harbour was hibernating and Sydney streets were sleeping. This is reflected in photos as often people and traffic are absent.

'Wealth is the ability to fully experience life.'
Henry David Thoreau

Experiencing Darling Harbour

The Goldsbrough building is located right on the doorstep of Darling Harbour foreshore.

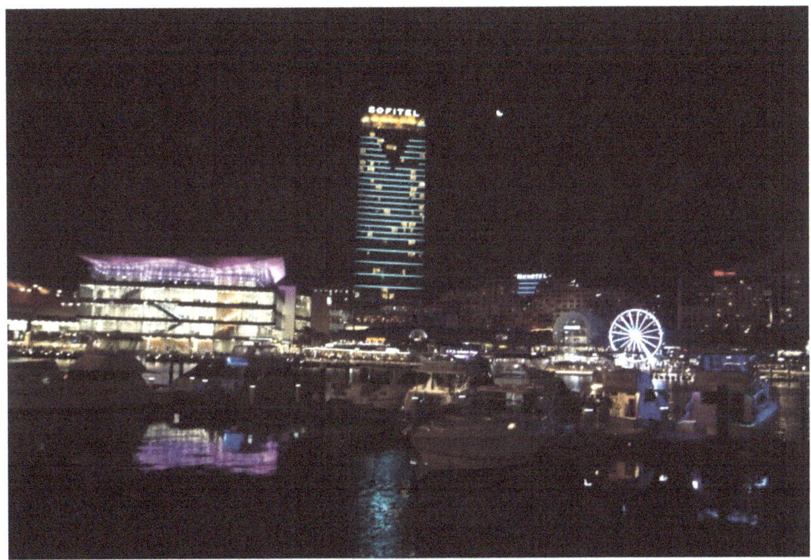

The Goldsbrough building (red brick with yellow entablature) as seen from the Pyrmont bridge.

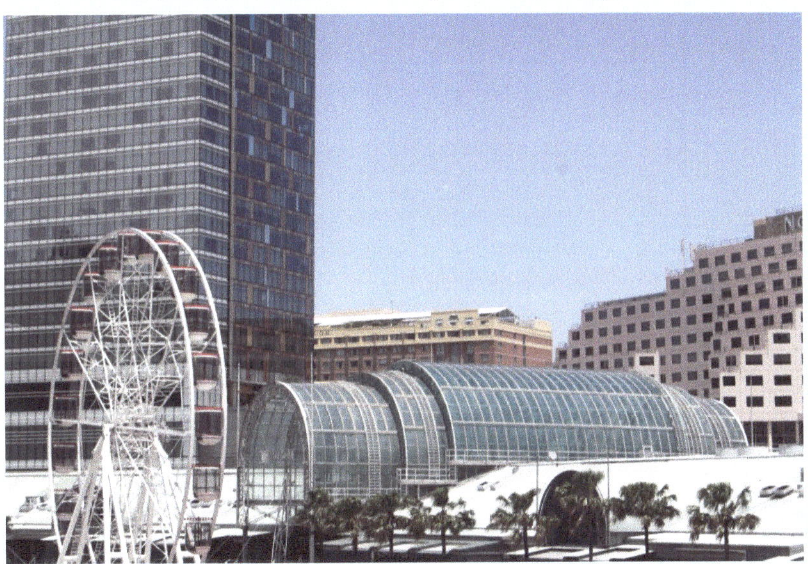

Darling Harbour was opened on 4 May 1988 by Queen Elizabeth II.

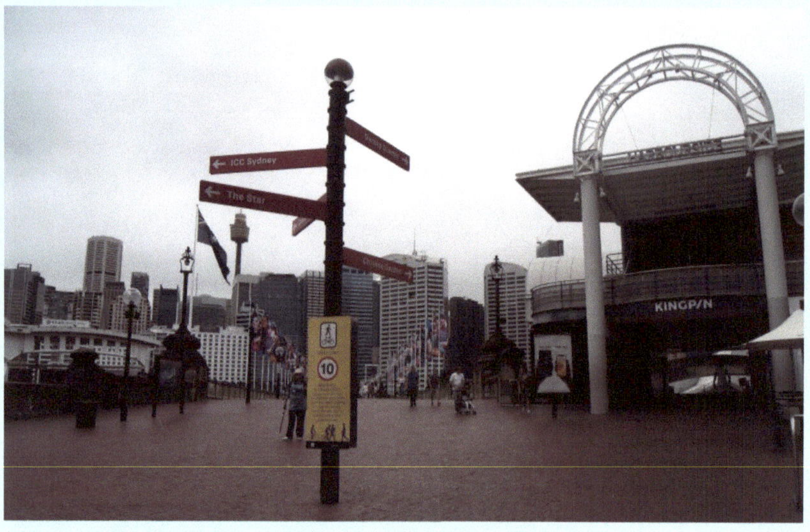

The Cockle Bay Wharf was constructed in 1998 when Darling Harbour celebrated its 10th birthday.

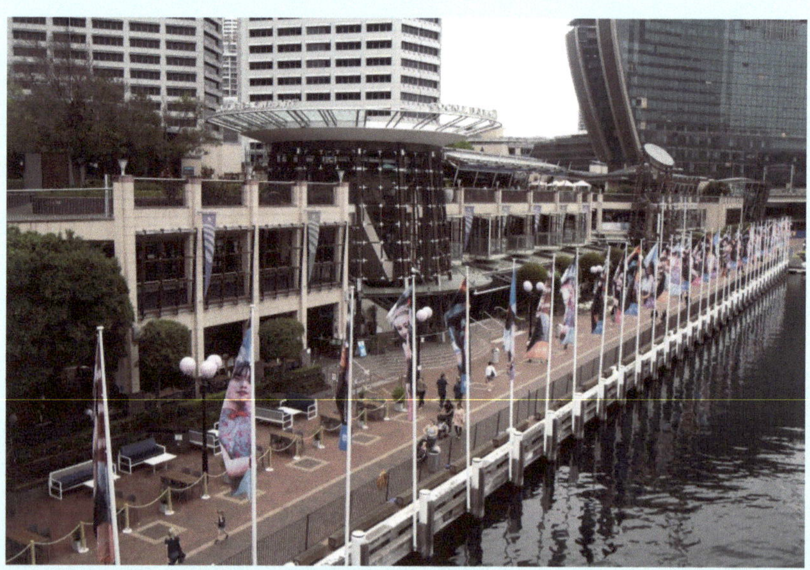

The **Sydney Aquarium** has more than 13,000 individual fish and other sea and water creatures from most of Australia's water habitats.

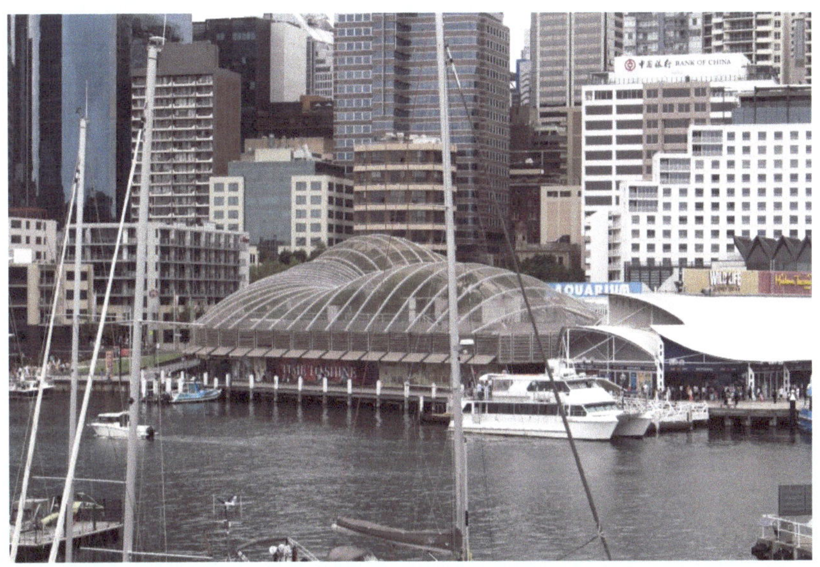

Restaurants and shopping centre

You can enjoy Australian, Asian, Brazilian, Chinese, European, French, German, Indian, Italian, Japanese, Mediterranean, Middle-Eastern, Seafood, Spanish, Thai, Vietnamese cuisines in many fine restaurants. There is also a food court inside the Harbourside shopping centre.

If you wish to dine on water, you can enjoy your meal in a floating restaurant while watching beautiful sceneries from the comfort of a large boat with live entertainment.

Apart from dining and shopping, Darling Harbour offers range of activities such as exhibitions, seminars, performing, water activities and the Darling Harbour Ferris Wheel can soar you up to 35 meters in the sky.

'The secret of change is to focus all of your energy, not on fighting the old, but on building the new.'
Socrates

Architecturally-renovated Apartment

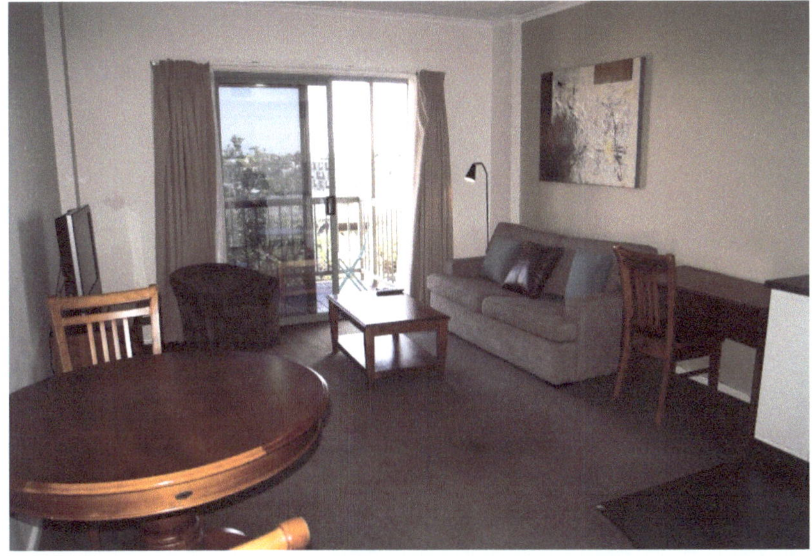

Our one bed-room apartment is located on level 11 of the beautiful and heritage-listed building.

It is a place to enjoy whether you are inside gazing into the distance or walking on the harbour or watching sunset on the water while busy people are ferrying home.

If you are here for business, the place is at a walking distance to the heart of Sydney with easy access to transport.

The pool and the gym will keep you fit.

‘I had three chairs in my house; one for solitude,
two for friendship, three for society.’
Henry David Thoreau

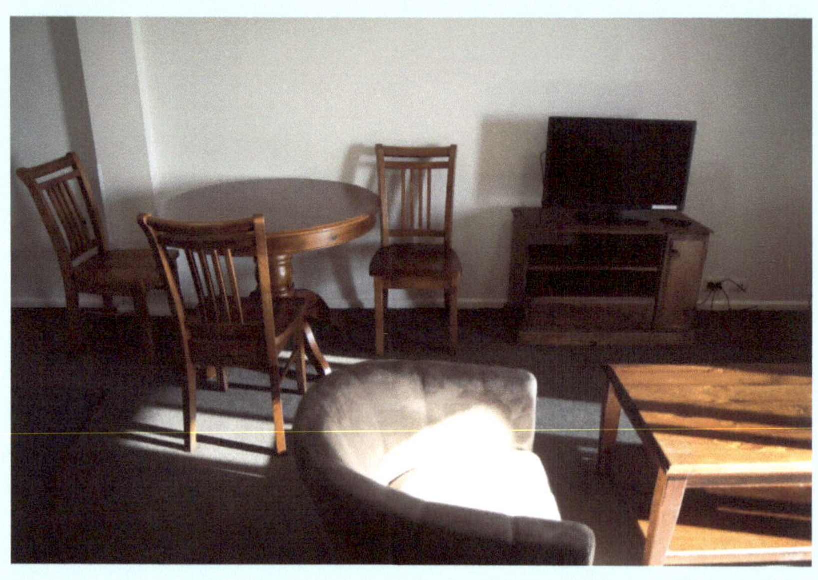

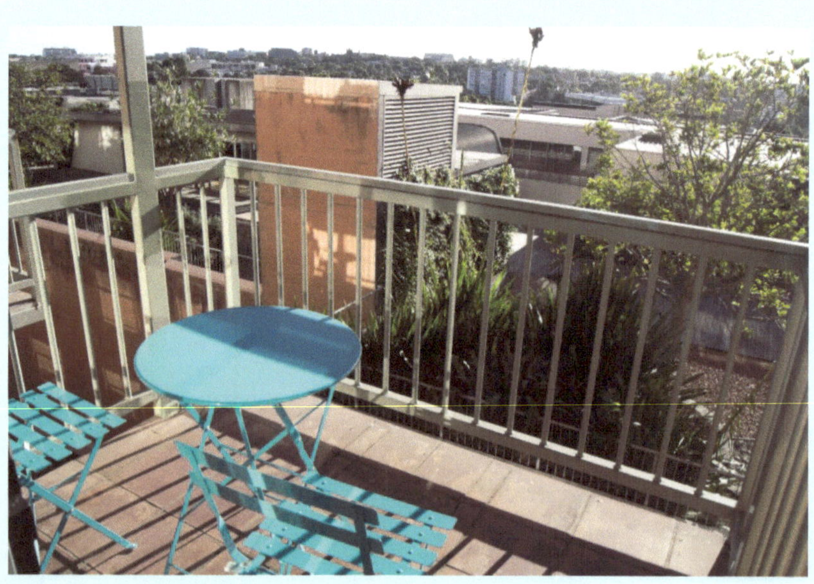

'Every sunset brings the promise of a new dawn.'
Ralph Waldo Emerson

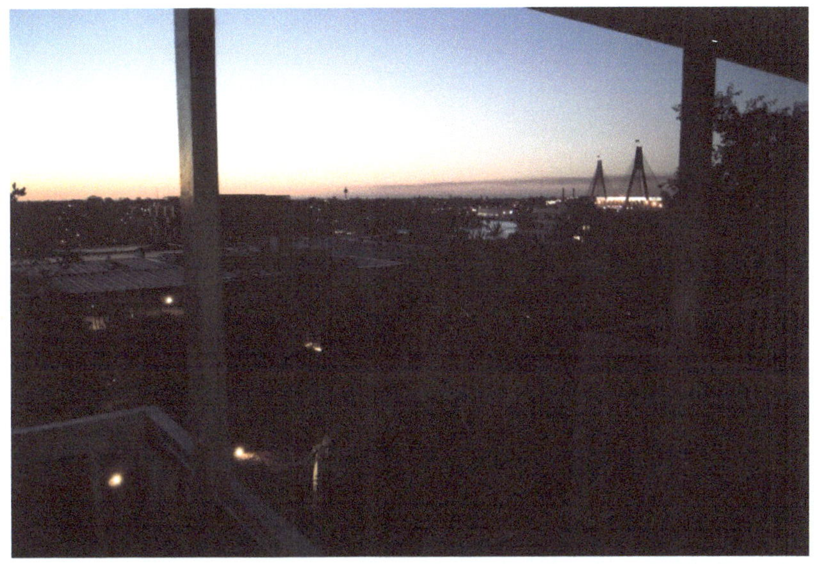

'One cannot think well, love well, sleep well,
if one has not dined well.' Virginia Woolf

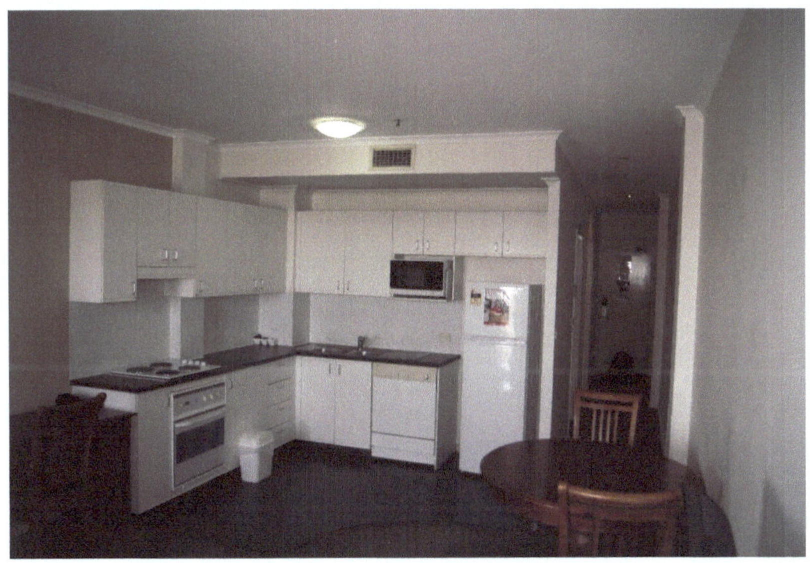

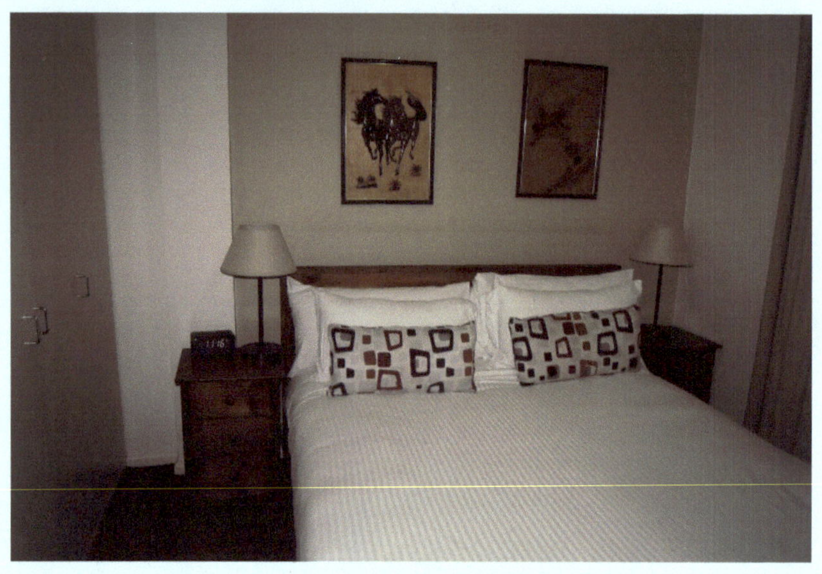

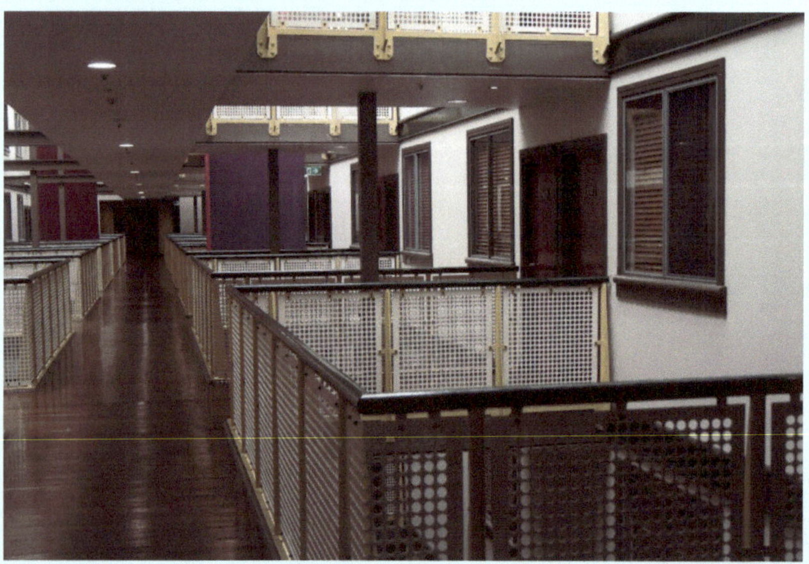

It is safe to leave your bedroom window open.

The two bed-room apartments, on level 11 and the penthouse floor, level 13, facing Darling Harbour, have views of Darling Harbour.

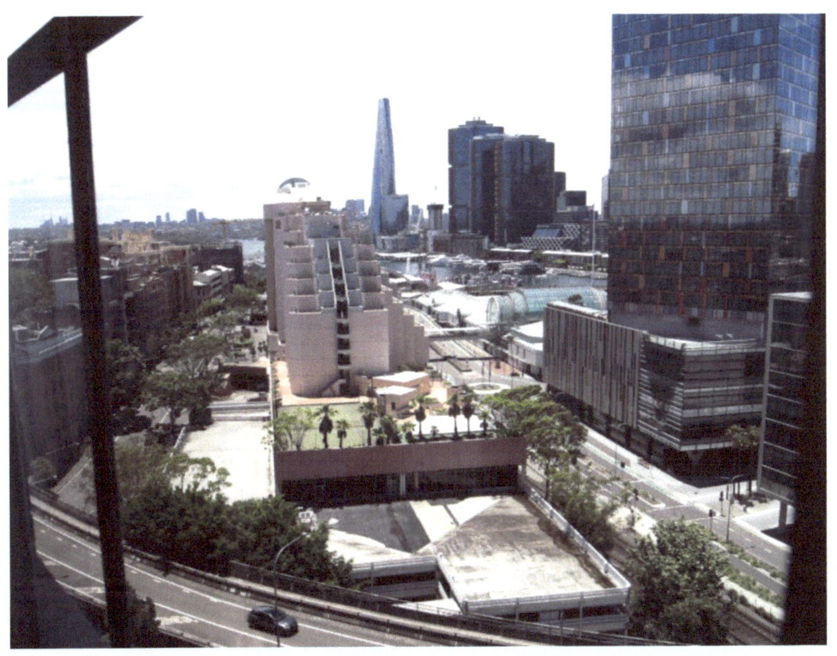

View from the lounge room window of our level 13
two-bedroom apartment.

'Love gives life to the lifeless.
Love lights a flame in the heart that is cold.
Love brings hope to the hopeless
and gladdens the hearts of the sorrowful.'
Abdu'l-Bahá

Love, Learn and Live

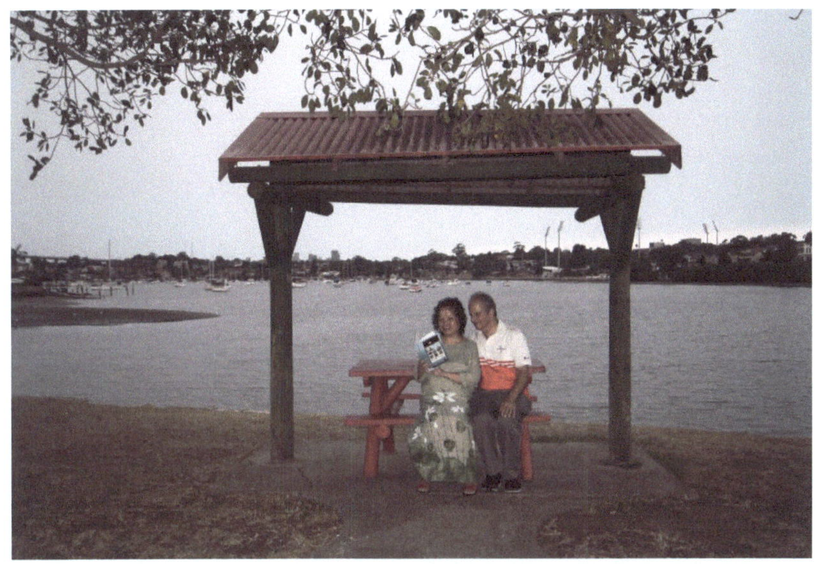

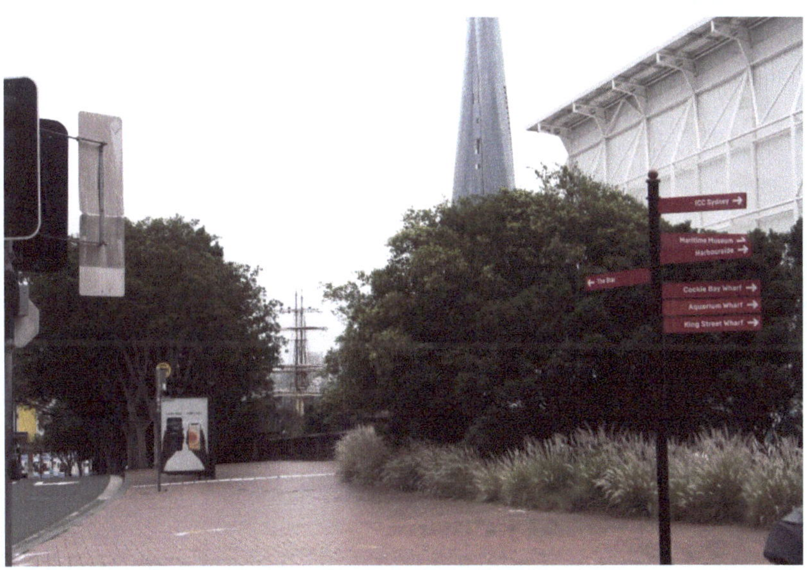

The Australian National Maritime Museum is an ideal place to visit either alone or with family. It is the only museum that is operated directly by the Federal government which is located outside the Australian Capital Territory. In 2010 it was listed as the 'World's 10 Coolest Museums' by the London Sunday Times.

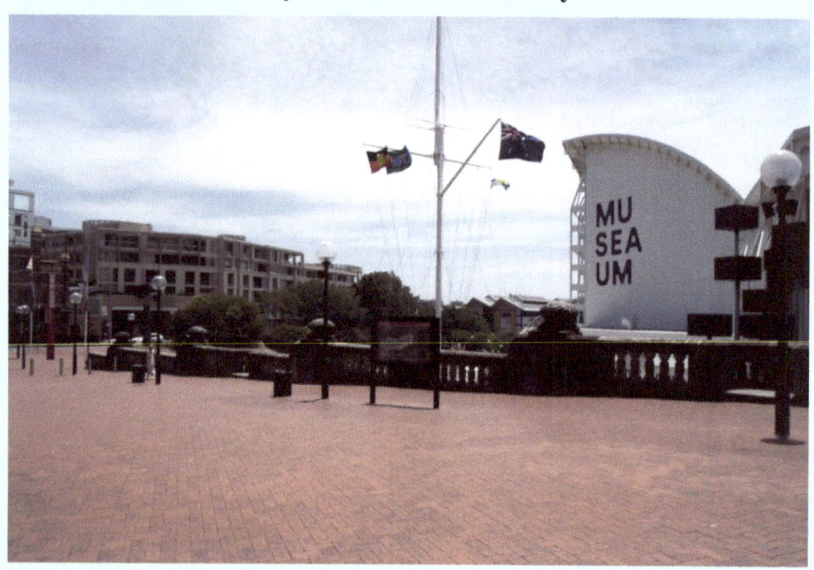

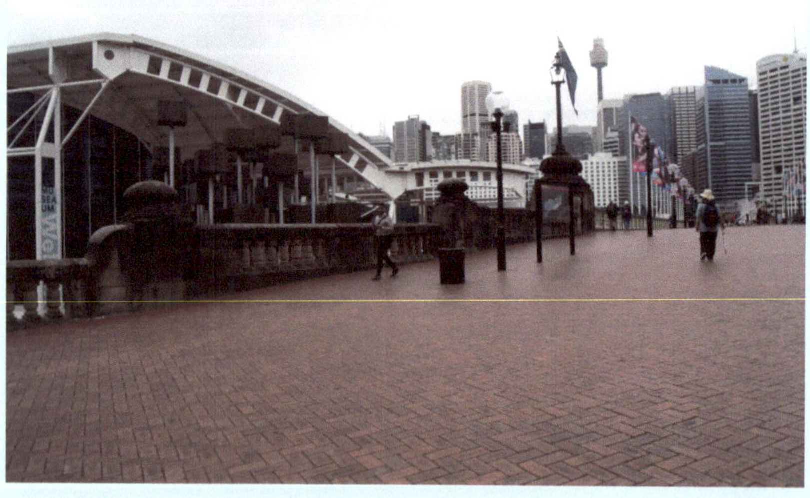

'Ships don't sink because of the water around them.
Ships sink because of the water that gets in them.
Don't let what's happening around you
get inside you and weigh you down.'
Author Unknown

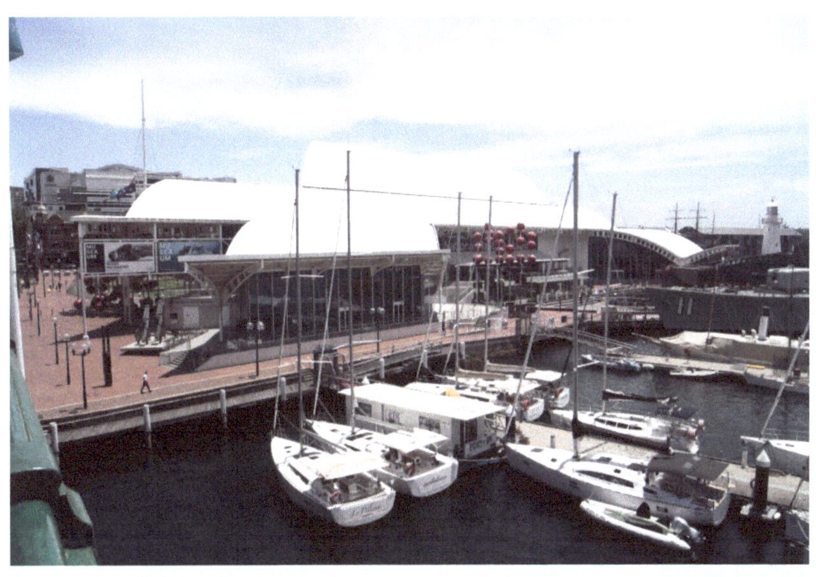

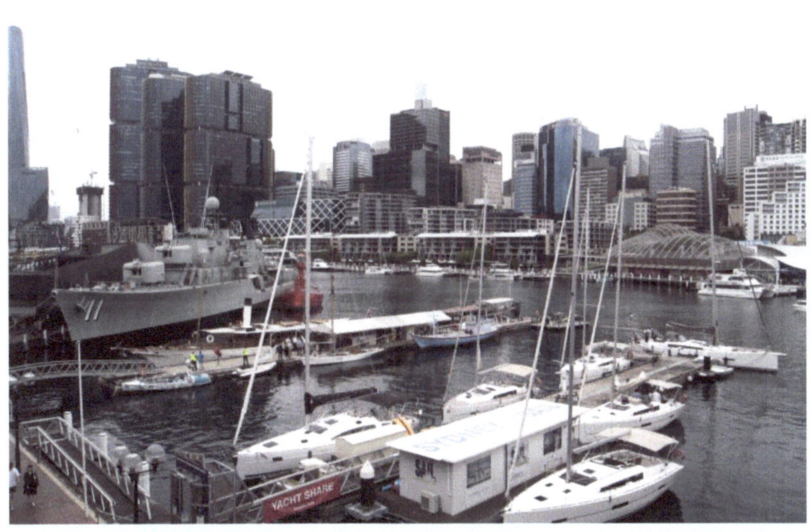

The International Convention Centre Sydney
(ICC Sydney) is Australia's second largest fully integrated
convention, exhibition and entertainment centre.

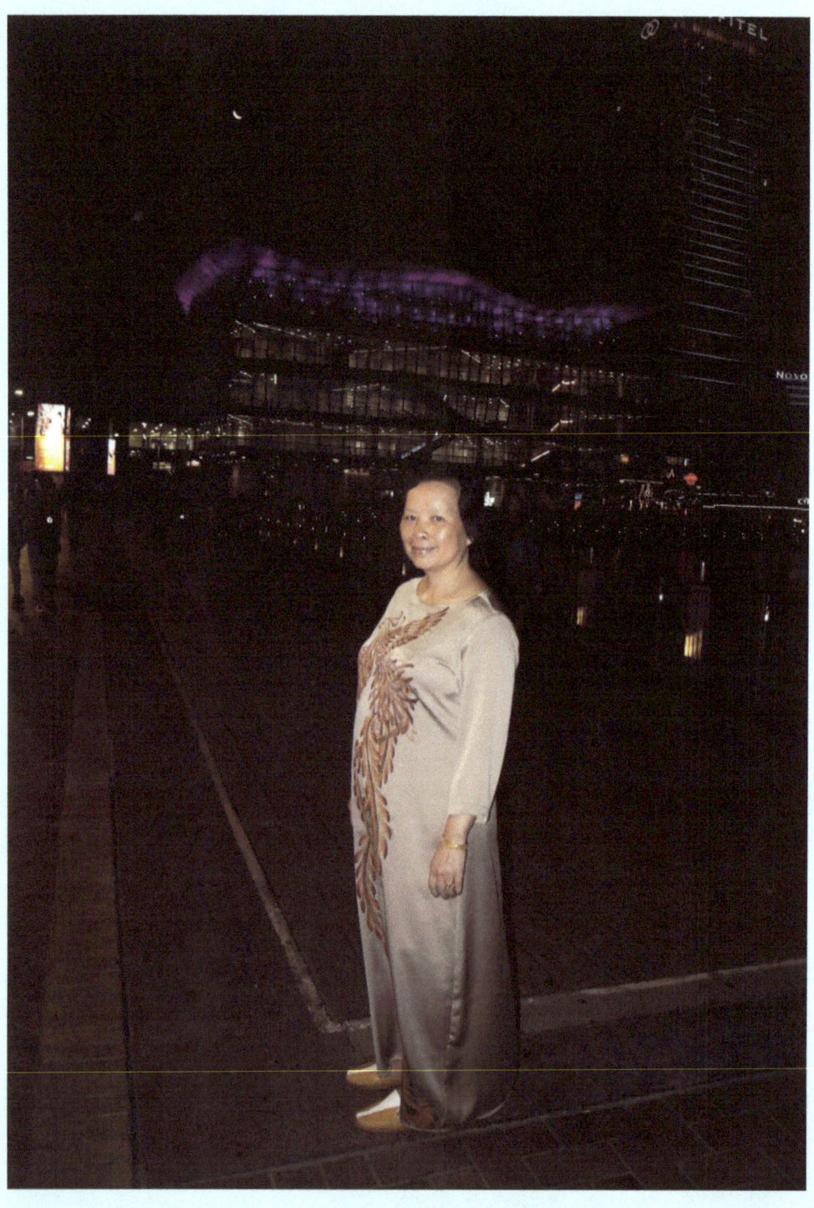

'Love is the bridge between you and everything.'
Rumi

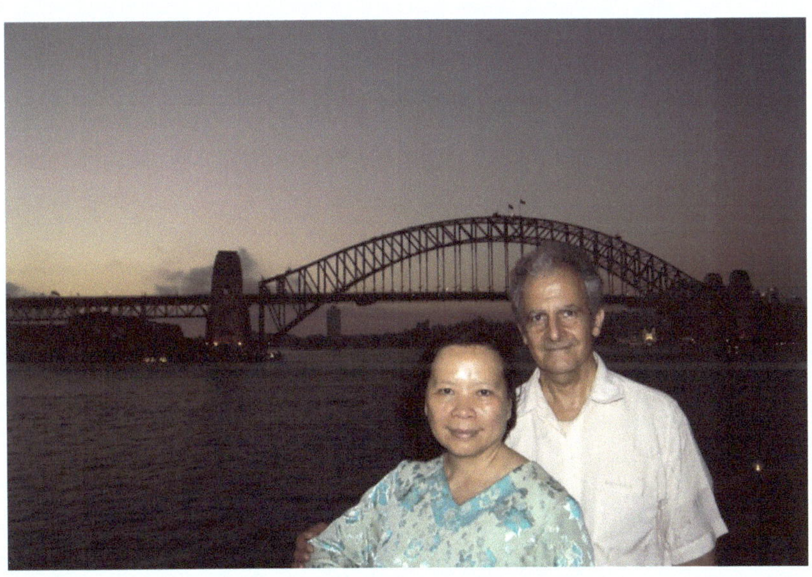

'Travel makes one modest.
You see what a tiny place
you occupy in the world.'
Gustave Flaubert

You can walk to the light rail station and Darling Harbour from the Goldsbrough building's entrance on level two.

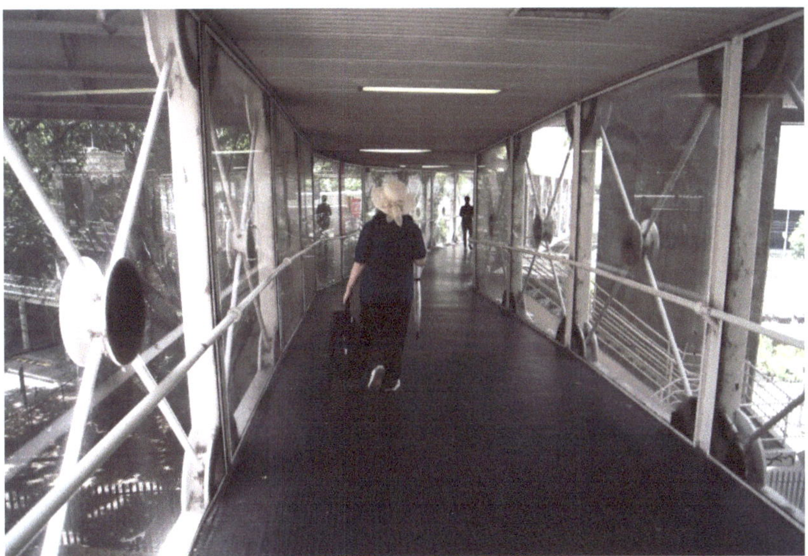

Overhead crossing over Pyrmont Street provides pathway through car park to the Darling Harbour.

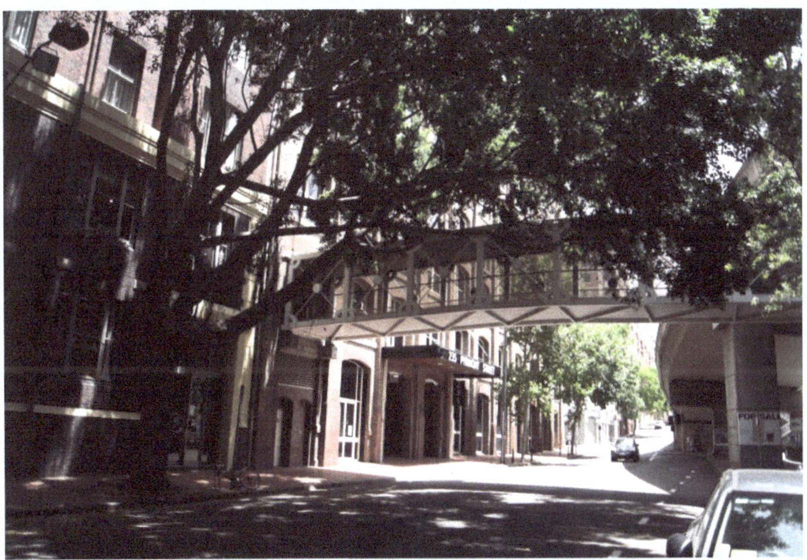

Light Train stopping at the Convention as viewed through the car park.

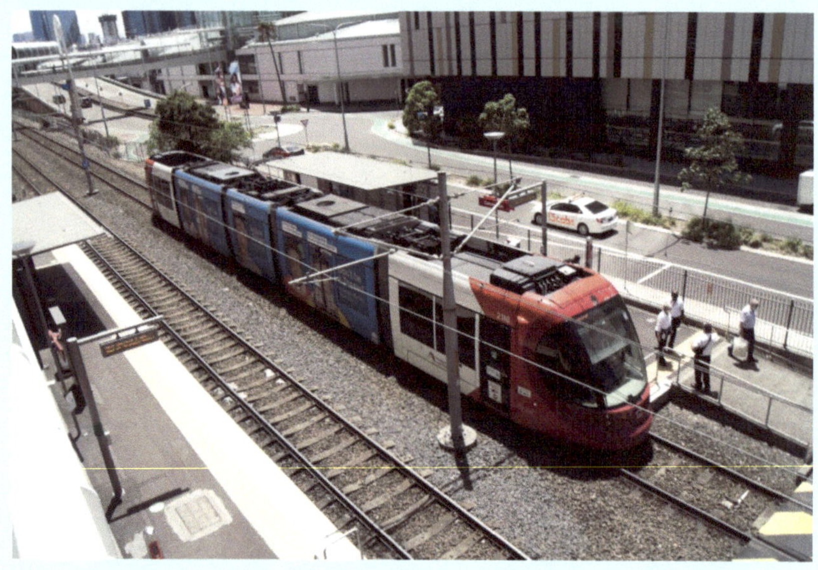

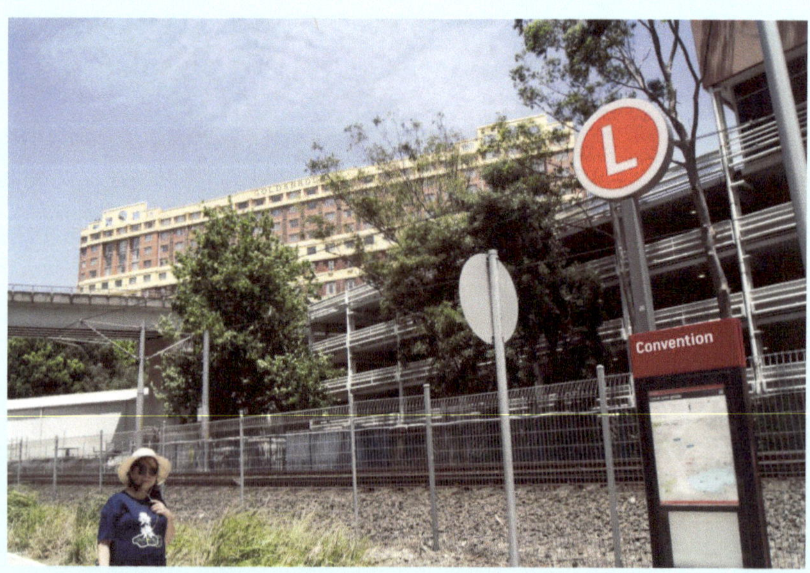

Darling Harbour footpath and restaurants.

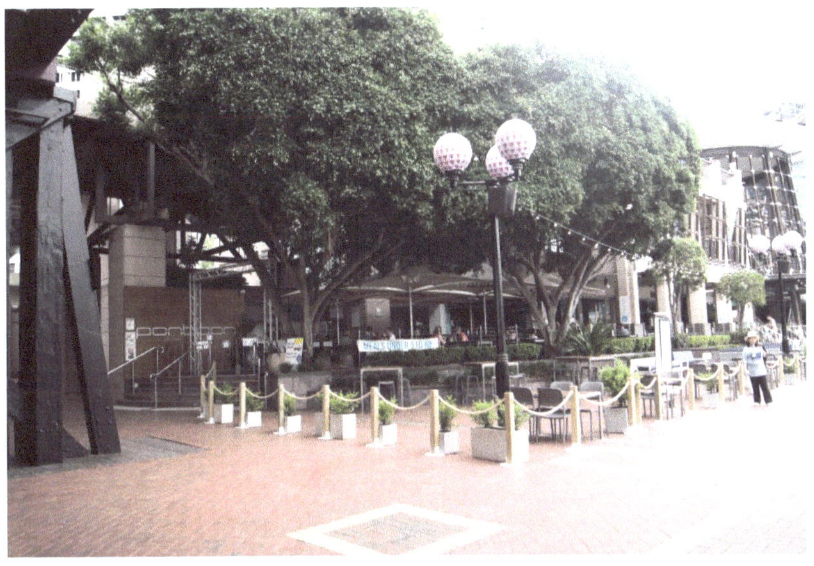

King Street Wharf on the eastern shore of Darling Harbour.

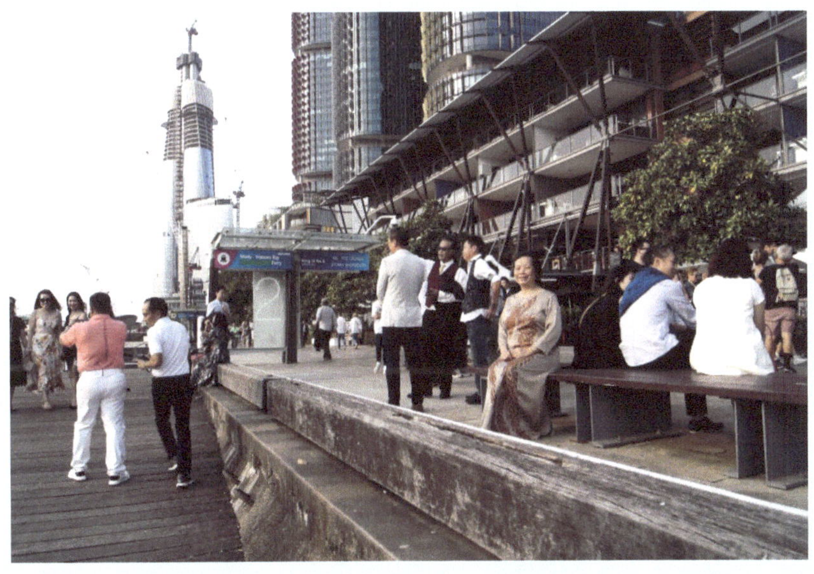

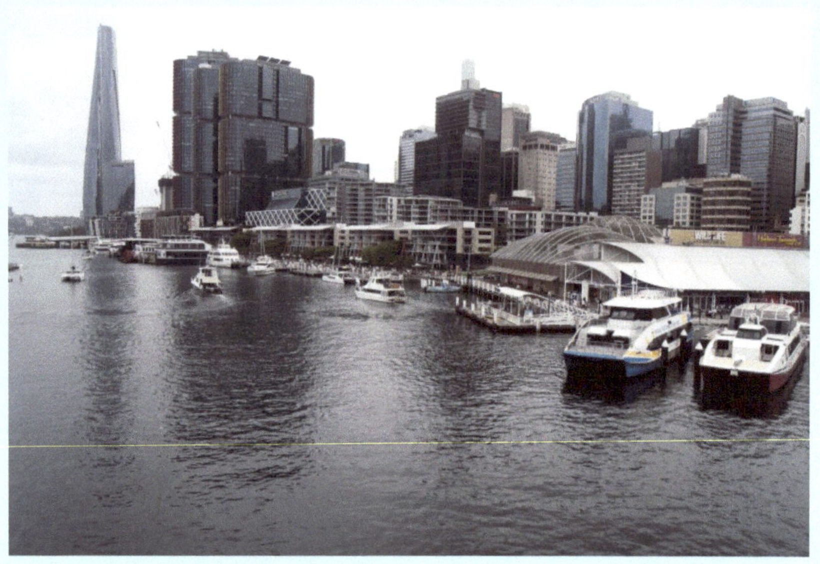

Dining on a boat is a pleasant way to see Sydney Habour.

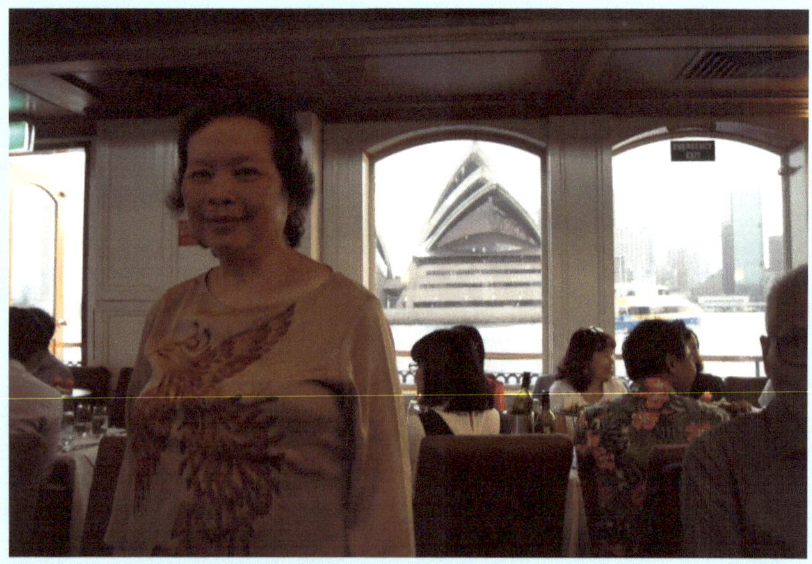

View from the boat: The **Sydney Harbour Bridge** is a heritage-listed steel through arch bridge. It was opened on 19 March 1932 by the Premier of NSW, Jack Lang.

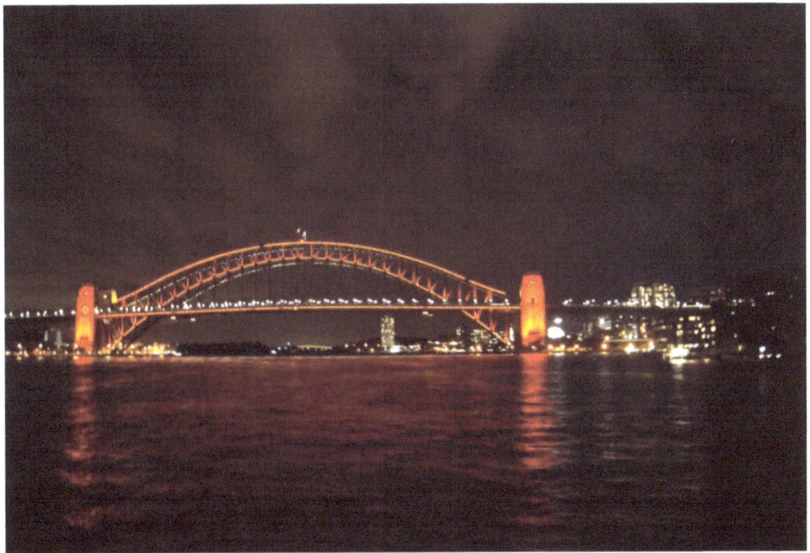

The **Sydney Opera House** is one of the 20th century's most famous and distinctive buildings. It was opened on 20 October 1973 by Queen Elizabeth II.

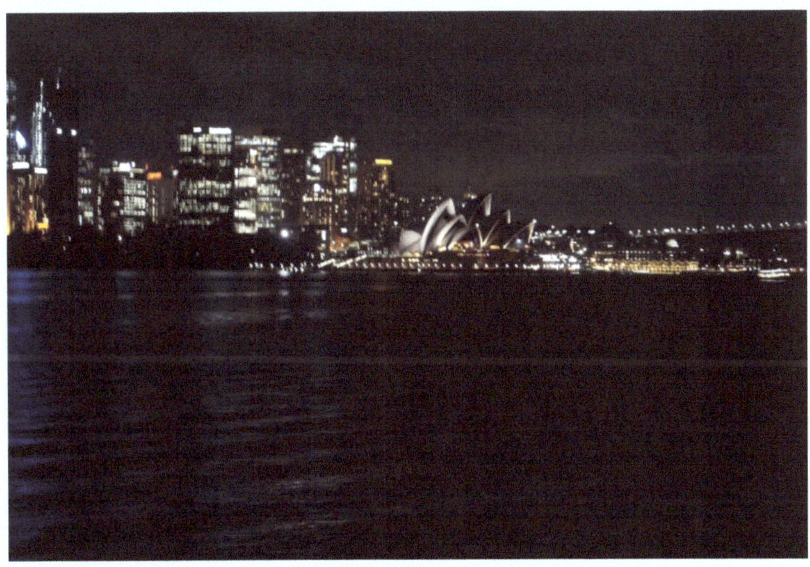

'Wherever you go,
go with all your Heart.'
Confucius

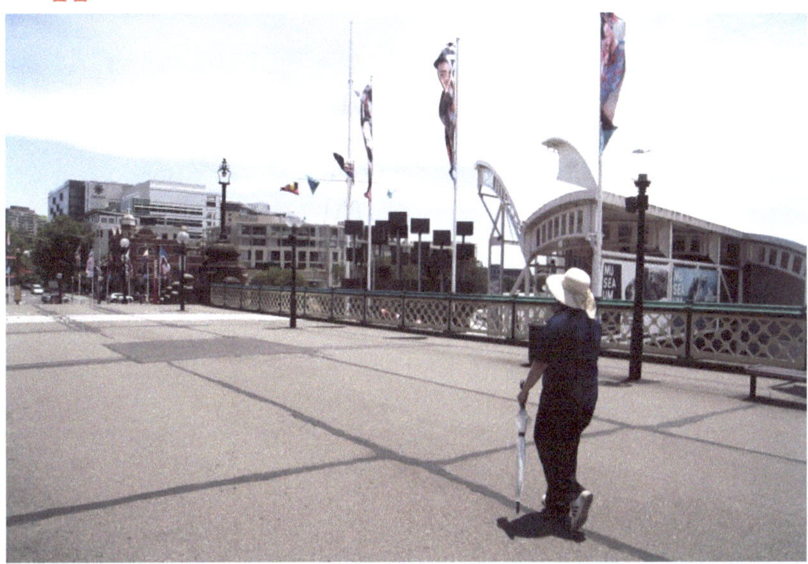

The Pyrmont Bridge is in the heart of Darling Harbour. It was opened in 1902, by the Governor of NSW Harry Rawson, to connect Sydney CBD with Pyrmont.

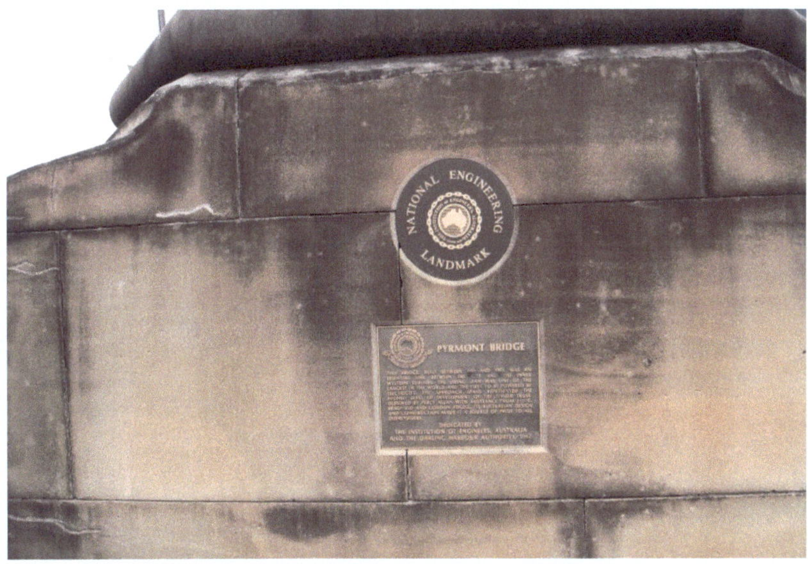

The Plaque of the Pyrmont Bridge.

The Pyrmont Bridge is the first and the oldest electrically powered swing span bridge in the world and it is still operating.

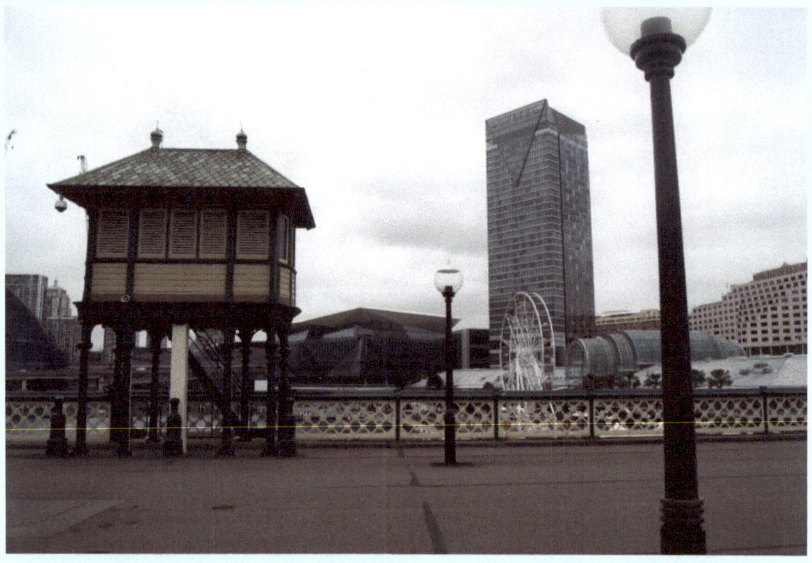

The bridge is a marvel and an Engineering Feat. The wooden exposed trusses show Australian workmanship.

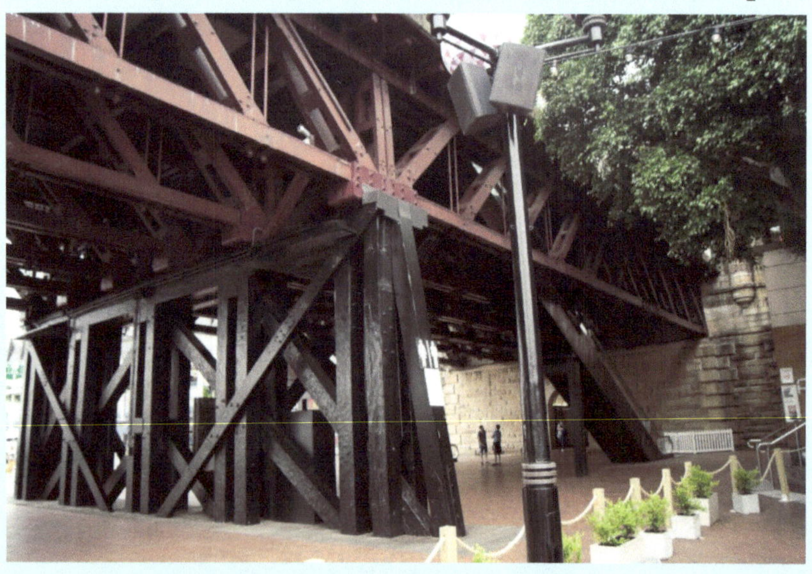

From the Pyrmont Bridge you can walk to Queen Victoria Building, Town Hall, Pitt Street Mall and Circular Quay.

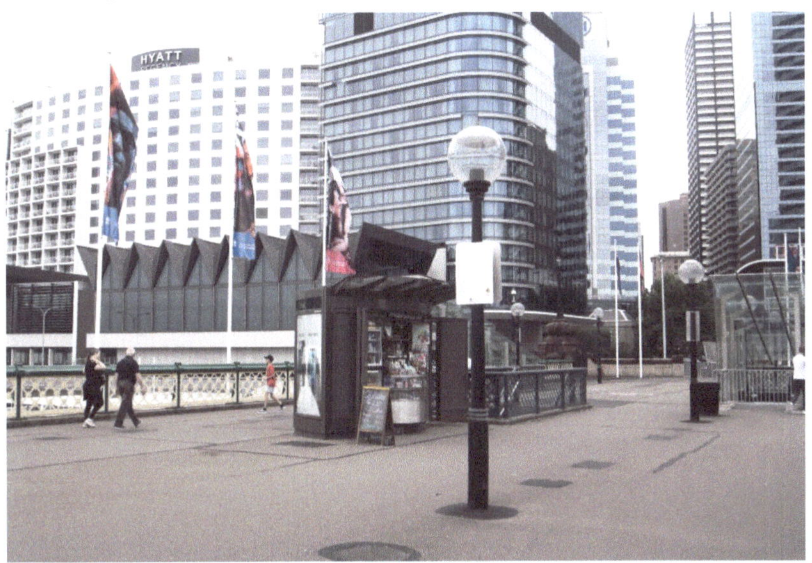

Market Street: A historic street with numerous historic buildings. A foot bridge connects Darling Harbour to Market Street, a glimpse of the Goldsbrough building.

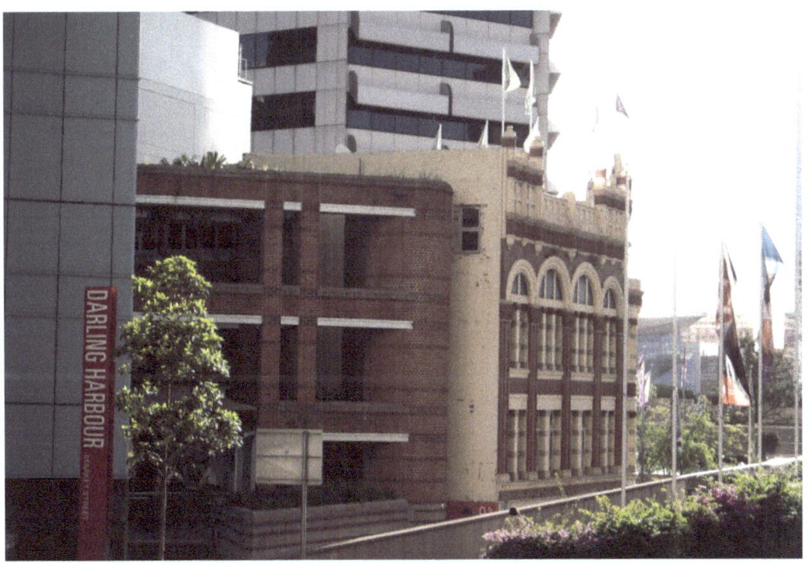

The former warehouse, 26 Market Street, has distinctive four gabled bays and high quality stone decoration.

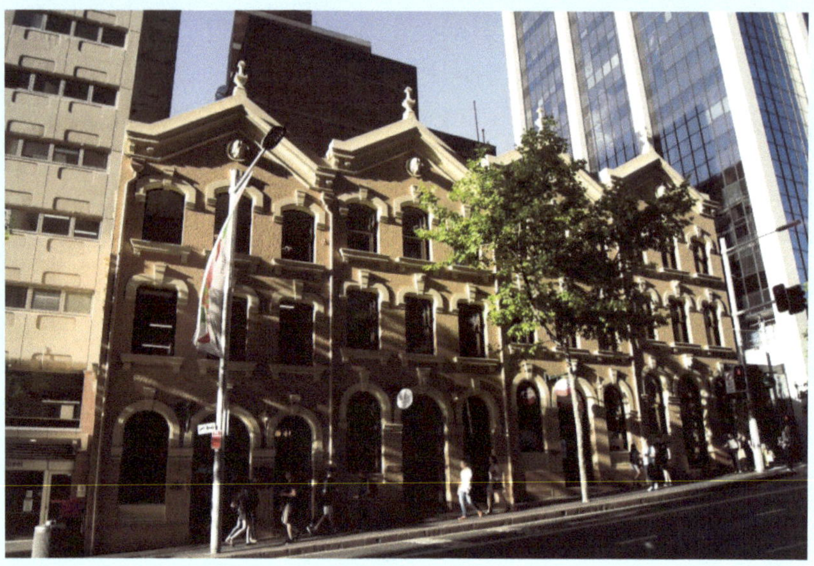

Queen Victoria Building: magnificent building in the Federation Romanesque style (or the American Romanesque style) built in 1893. The sandstones were quarried from Darling Harbour.

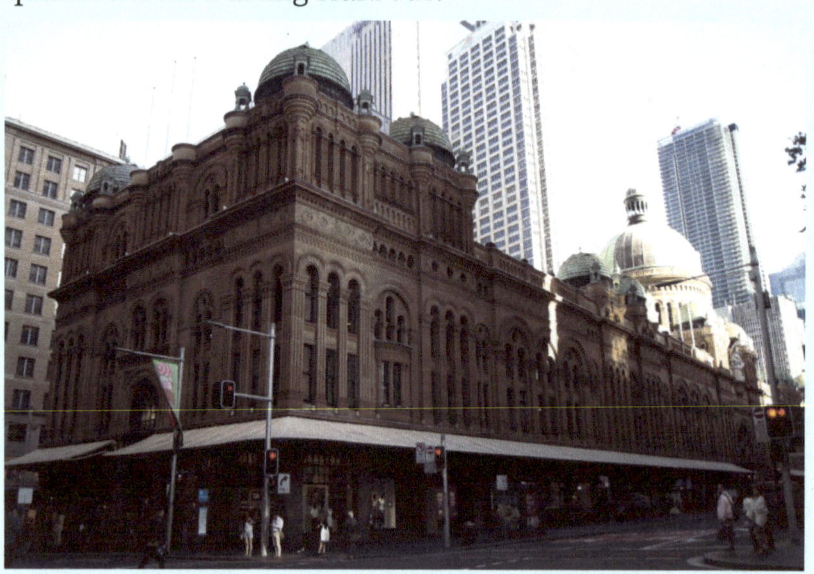

Queen Victoria building is one of the best and most beautiful boutique shopping centers in Sydney.

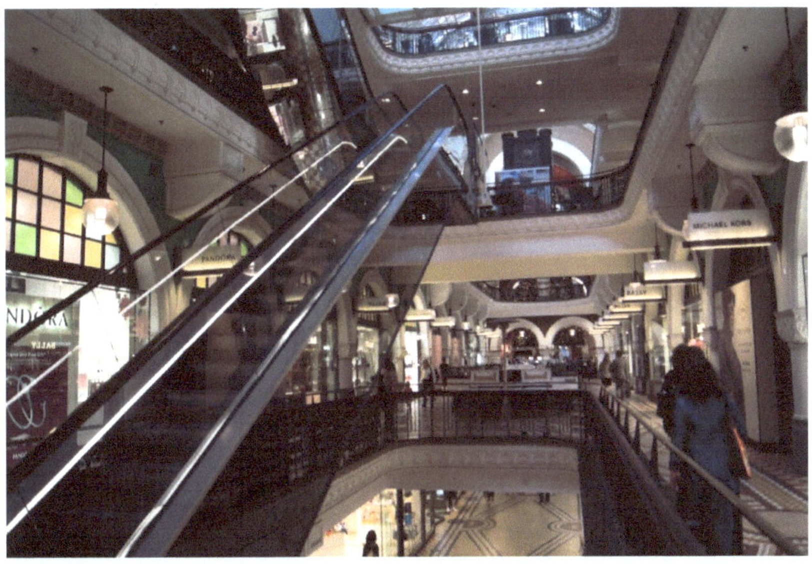

Queen Victoria's Dog, *Islay*, in the shadow of her Majesty's statue, solicits coins for deaf and blind children and guards the wishing well in front of the building.

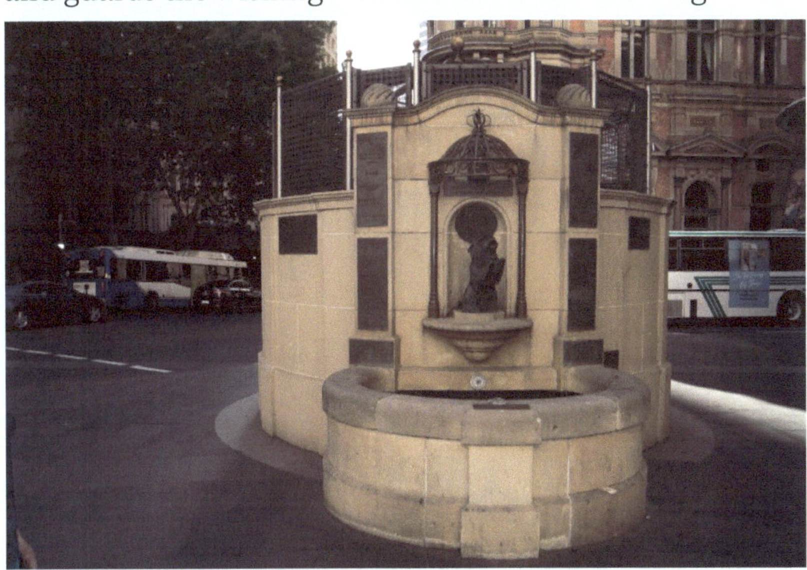

'O Queen in London!

... We have been informed that thou hast forbidden the trading in slaves, both men and women. This, verily, is what God hath enjoined in this wondrous Revelation. God hath, truly, destined a reward for thee, because of this ...
We have also heard that thou hast entrusted the reins of counsel into the hands of the representatives of the people. Thou, indeed, hast done well, for thereby the foundations of the edifice of thine affairs will be strengthened, and the hearts of all that are beneath thy shadow, whether high or low, will be tranquillized. It behoveth them, however, to be trustworthy among His servants, and to regard themselves as the representatives of all that dwell on earth ...'

Extracts from the Tablet of Bahá'u'lláh
addressed to Queen Victoria.

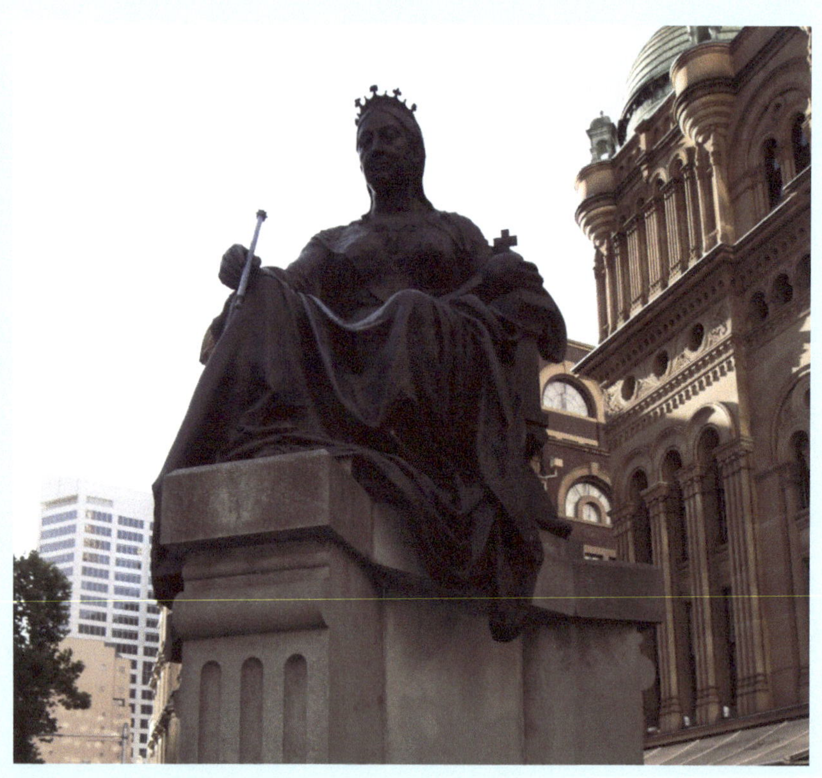

An ornate 1890 building that used to be a hotel is alongside of the Queen Victoria building, in the corner of York and Druitt streets.

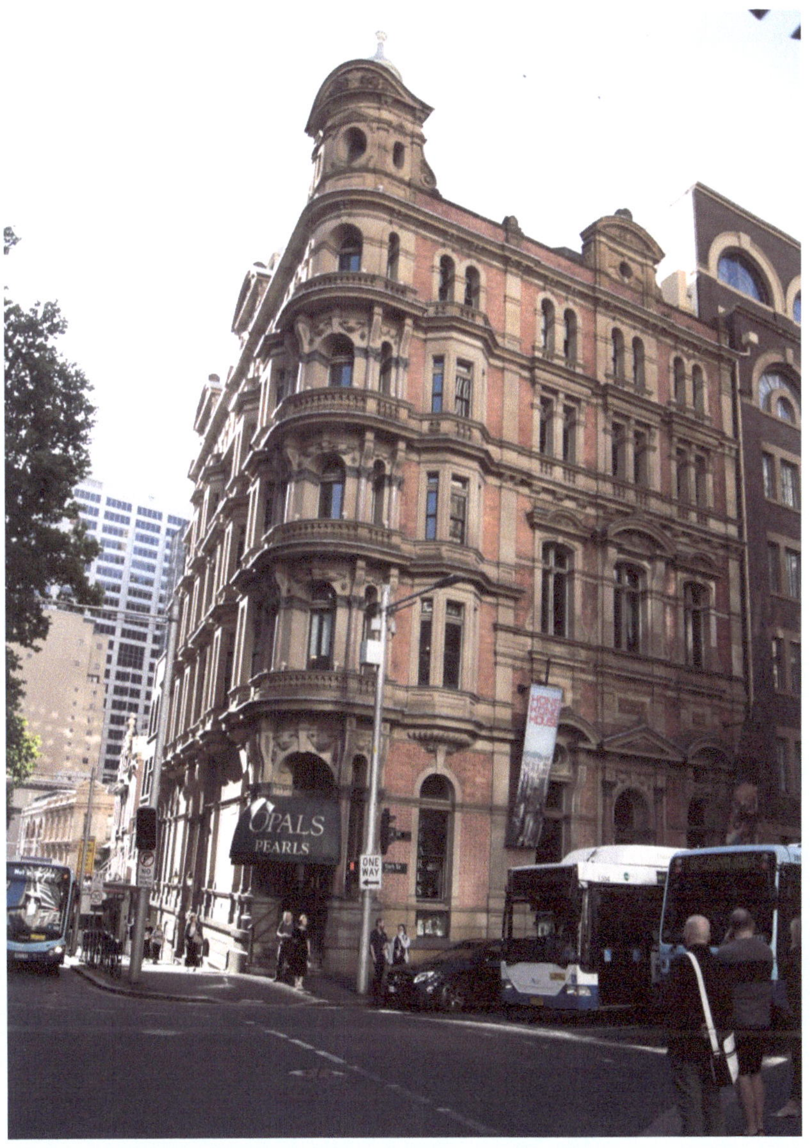

Within walking distance there are numerous heritage listed buildings which are marvels of the last century architecture.

Town Hall is another architectural landmark with its sandstones from Darling Harbour.

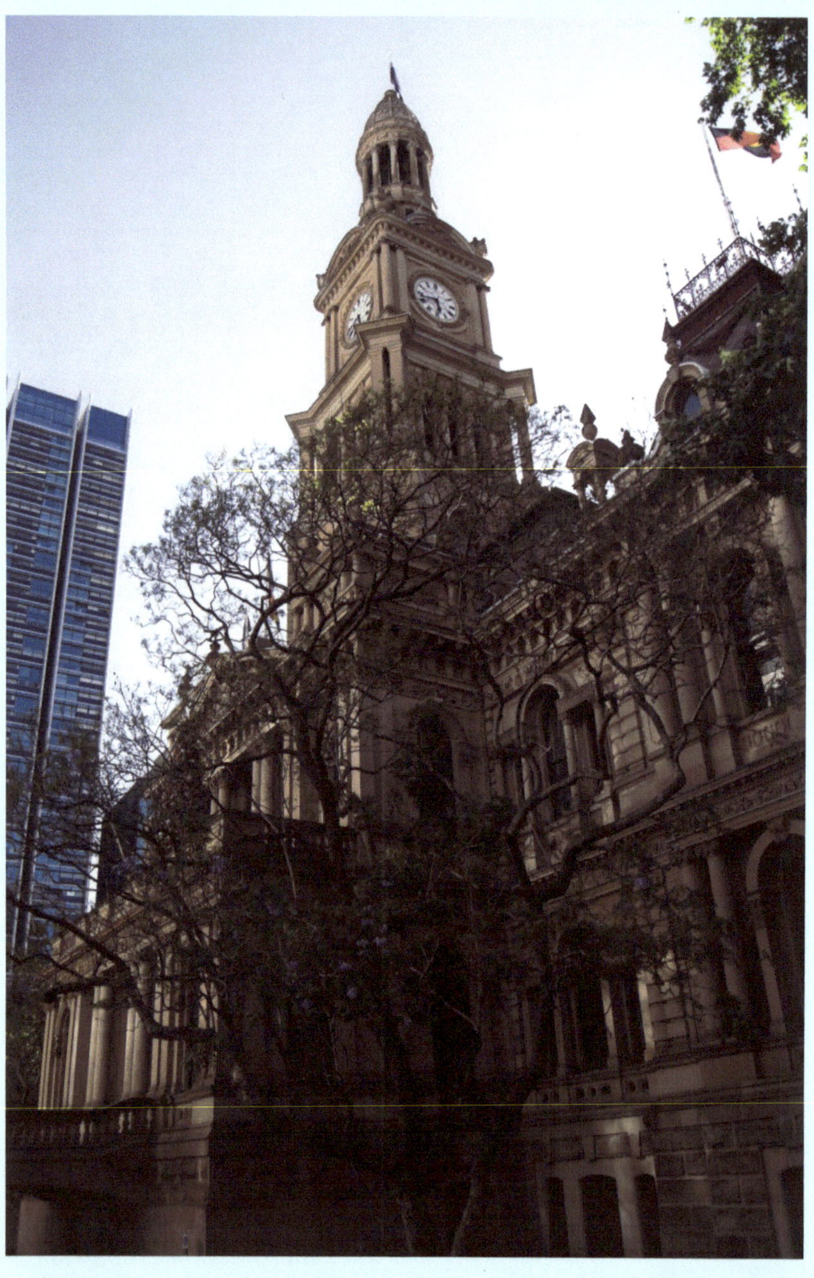

'You yourself,
as much as anybody in the entire universe,
deserve your love and affection.'
Buddha

'Walking is the best possible exercise.
Habituate yourself to walk very far.'
Thomas Jefferson

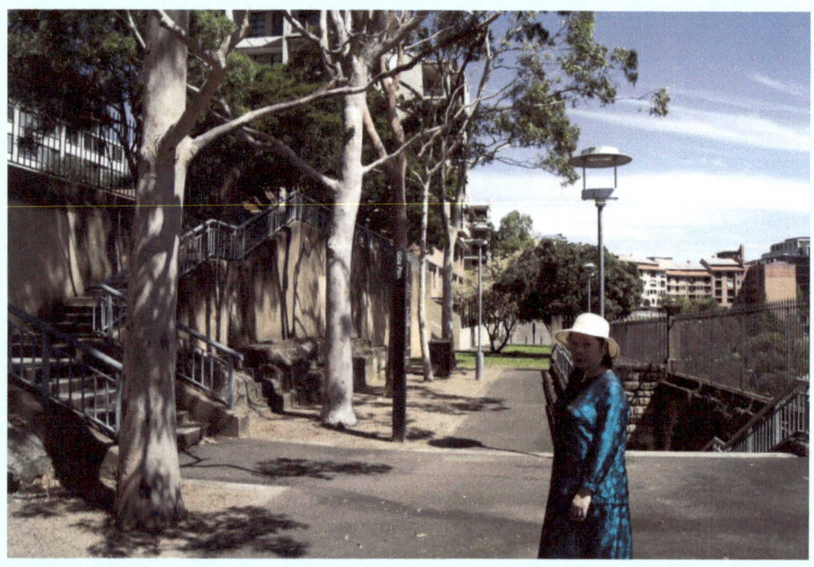

'All life is an Experiment.
The more Experiments you make the better.'
Ralph Waldo Emerson

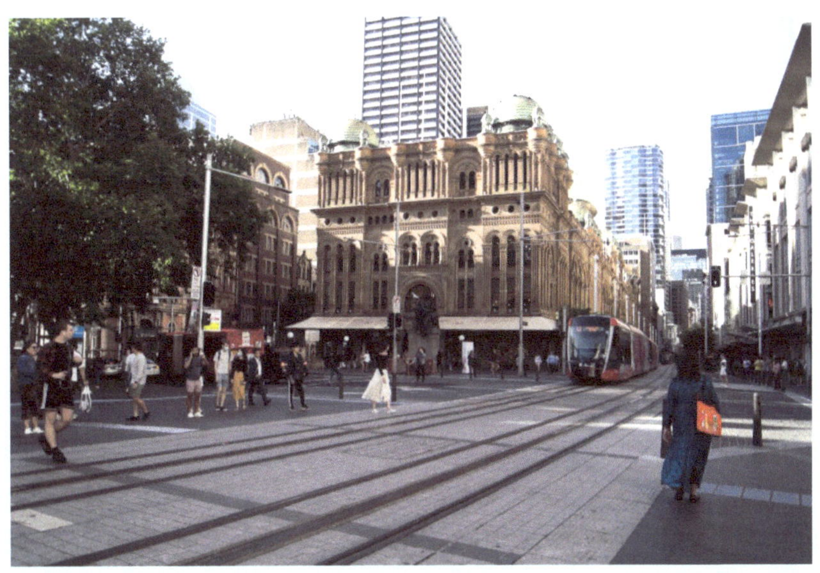

'Architecture aims at eternity.'
Christopher Wren

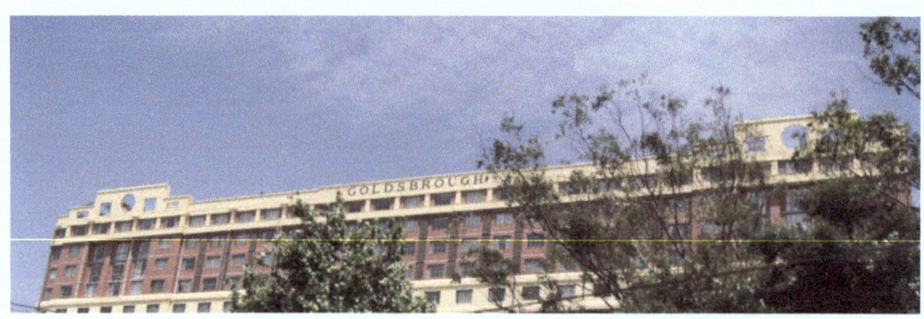

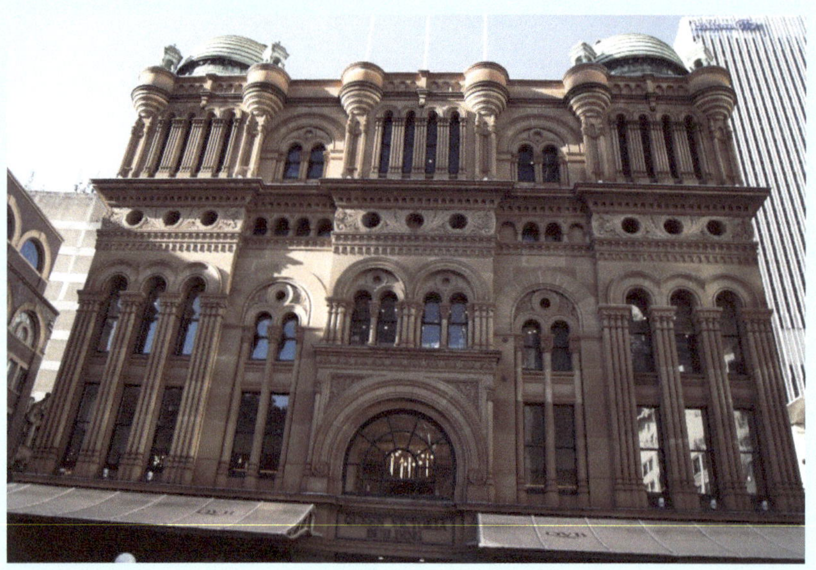

'In the world of existence there is indeed
no greater power than the power of Love.'
Abdu'l-Bahá

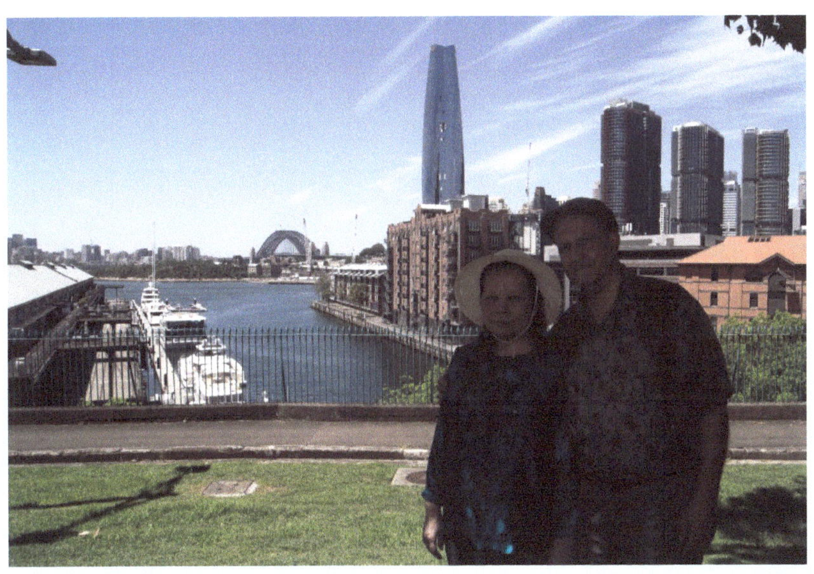

'Three things cannot be long hidden:
the Sun, the Moon, and the Truth.'
Buddha

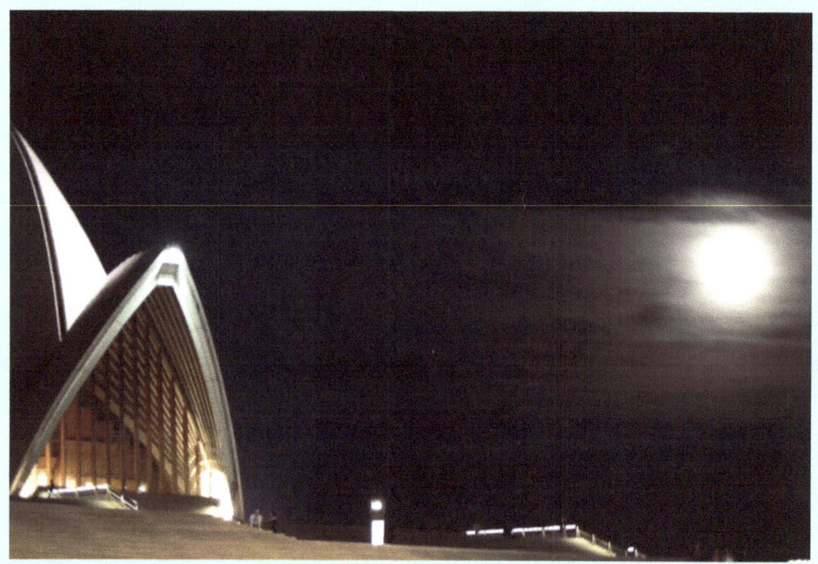

H

'Health is the greatest gift,

contentment the greatest wealth,

faithfulness the best relationship.'

Buddha

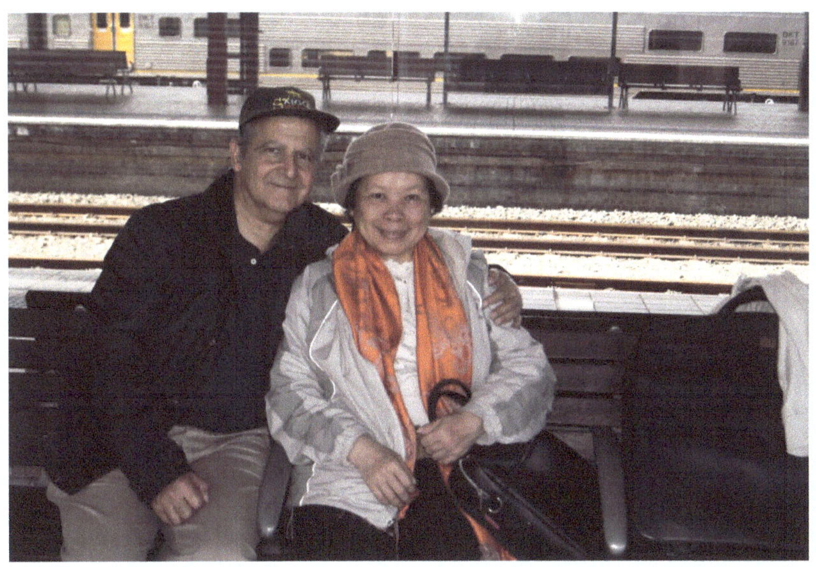

'be Yourself not your idea of what you think
somebody else's idea of yourself should be.'
Henry Ford

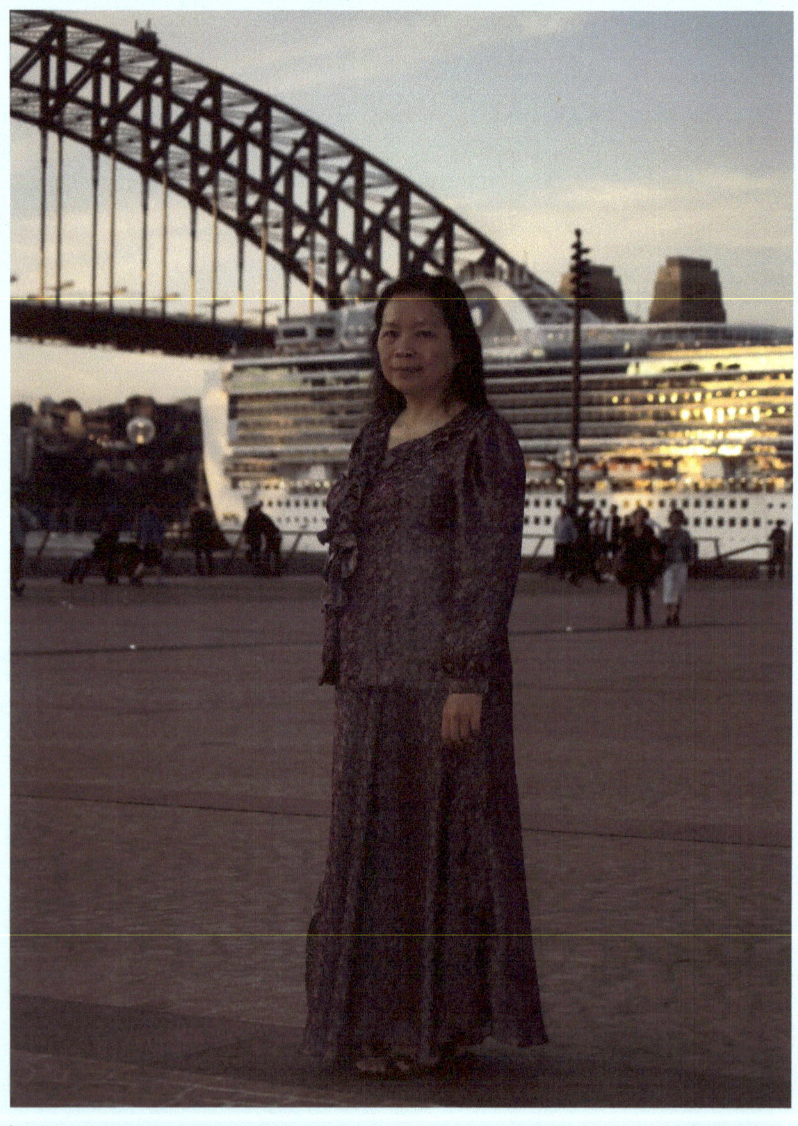

'be Yourself not your idea of what you think

Mind

'Your Mind is a powerful thing.
When you filter it with positive thoughts,
your life will start to change.'
Buddha

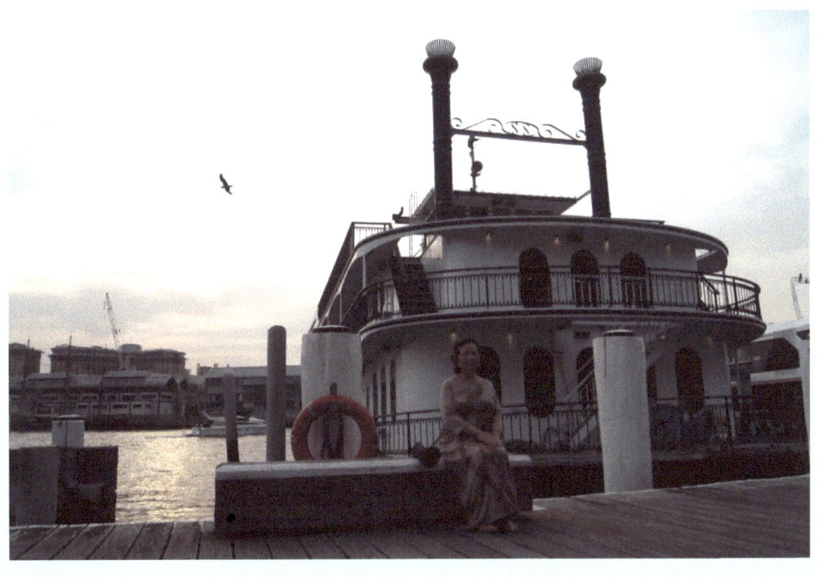

Enthusiasm

'Enthusiasm is one of the most powerful engines
of success.
When you do a thing, do it with all your might.
Put your whole soul into it.
Stamp it with your own personality.
Be active, be energetic, be enthusiastic and
faithful, and you will accomplish your object.
Nothing great was ever achieved without
Enthusiasm.'
Ralph Waldo Emerson

Goldsbrough Building

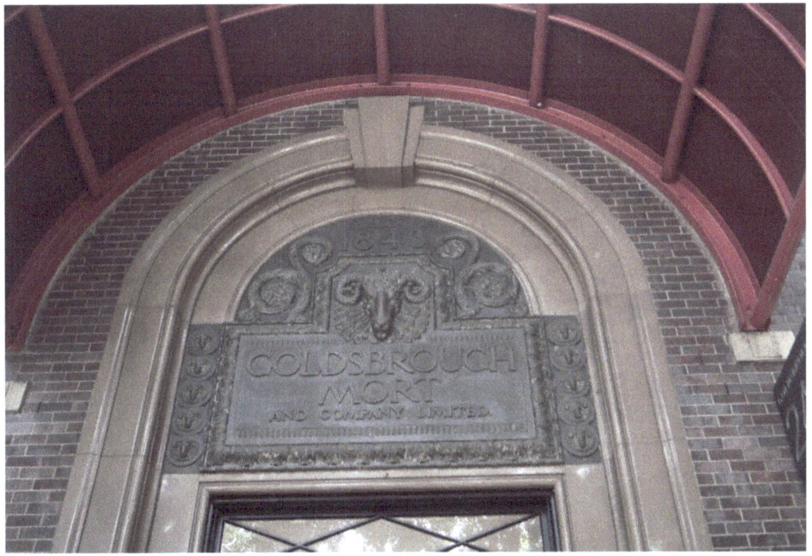

The Goldsbrough building is named after Richard Goldsbrough who was born on 17 October 1821 in Yorkshire, the only son of Joshua Goldsbrough, a butcher, and his wife Hannah, née Speight. He sailed from England in 1847 to Australia and arrived in 1848. He passed away from an internal tumour on 8 April 1886.

Goldsbrough is an Anglo-Saxon surname. Historically, surnames evolved as a way to sort people into groups. Goldsbrough was given to a goldsmith or a jeweller refiner or a gilder. The surname Goldsbrough was first found at Goldsborough, a parish near Knaresborough, West Riding of Yorkshire, meaning 'the borough of Gold.'

Mr Goldsbrough played an important role in the development of the Australian wool trade during the 19th century. Today Australia is one of the largest wool producers in the world.

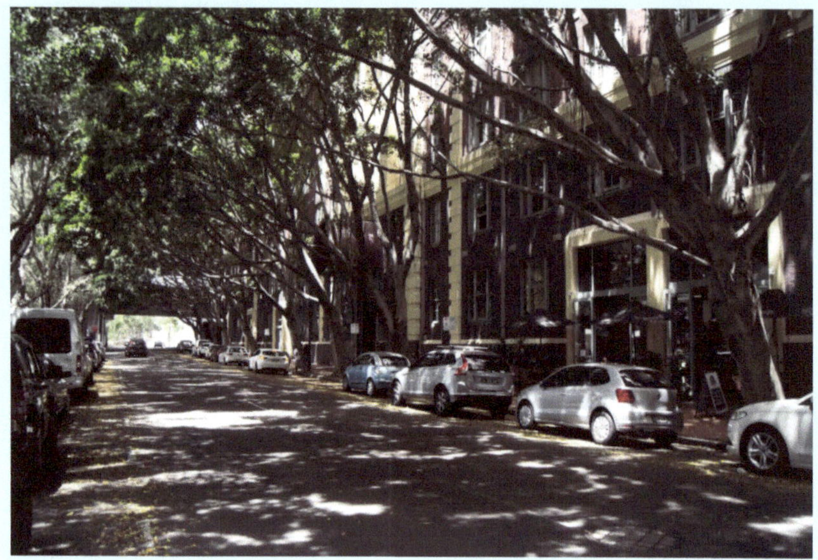

The original Goldsbrough building was constructed between 1881 and 1883 as a large wool store. The building was built near the port to allow for storage of wool carted to it by train and waited to be loaded onto the ships bound for England. In 1922, three floors were added. The Goldsbrough building played an important role in the development of Darling Harbour as a commercial port and the railway systems in Pyrmont. The wool store was of such importance that when on 25 September 1935 it was destroyed by fire, it was immediately rebuilt and operational in 1936. Gradually the ships went away and the port disappeared and the last train blew its whistle one last time before it disappeared from Pyrmont.

There was no more wool to store. But now the lovely wooden beams and trusses have precious gems to store, the people who would love to live within its walls. In 1995, the Goldsbrough building was converted into self-contained studio, one and two bed-room apartments and penthouses with all the amenities that modern men and woman consider essential to living: an onsite gym, an indoor heated swimming pool, shops, offices and eateries.

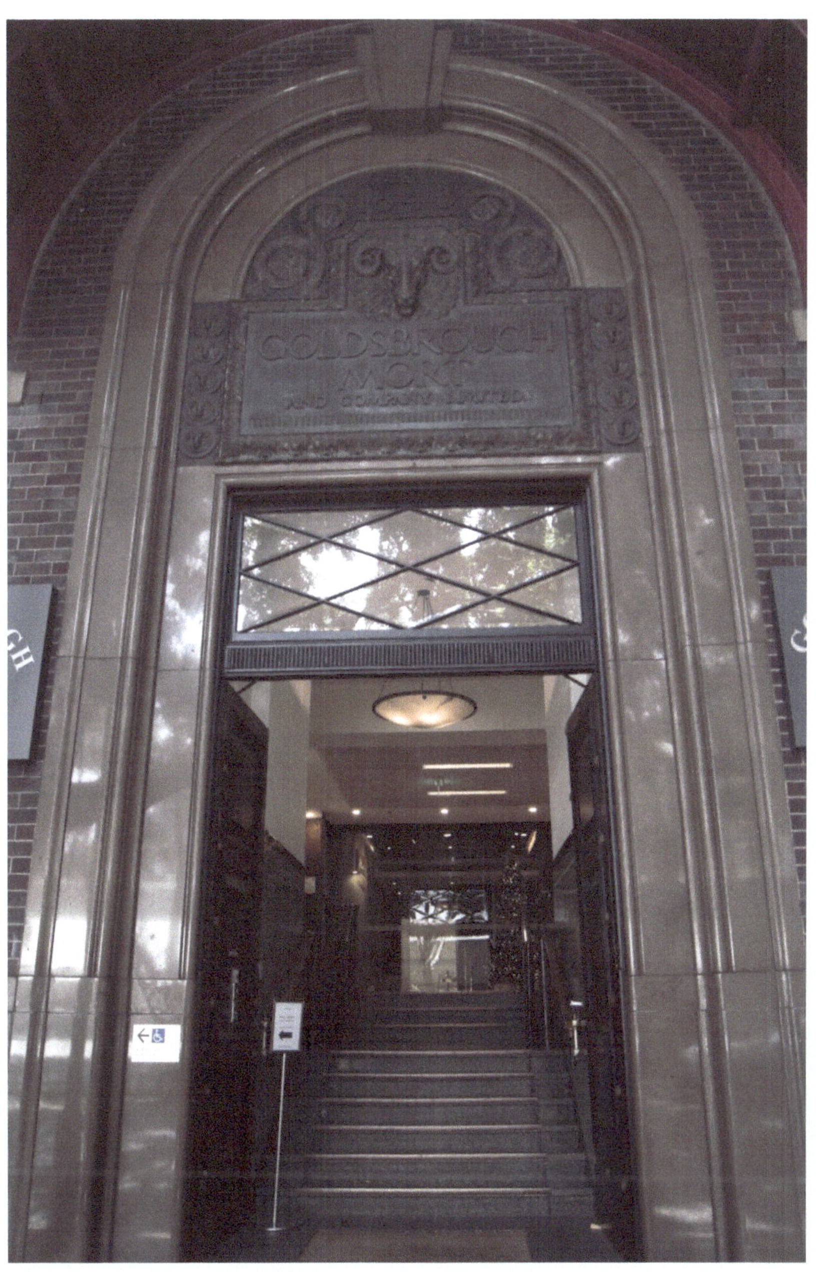

The Goldsbrough building has an impressive neo-classical façade with original timber floors and unique exposed ironbark columns.

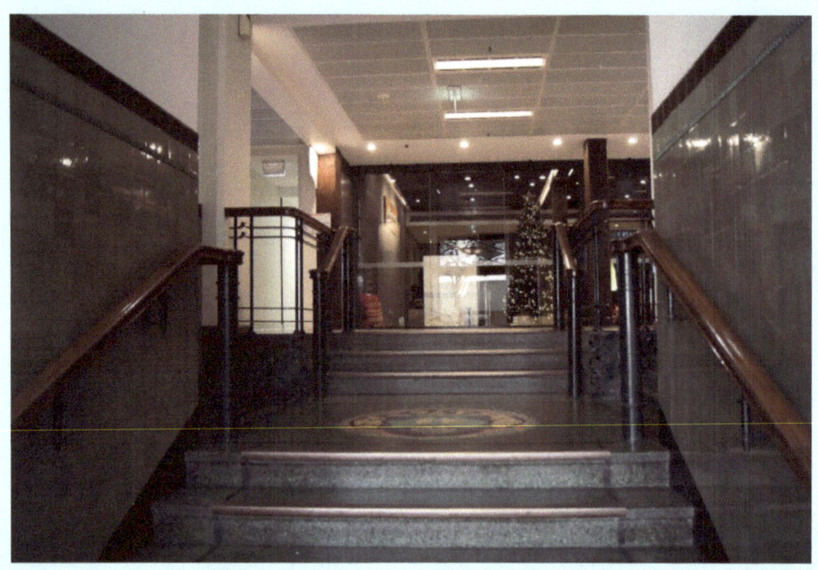

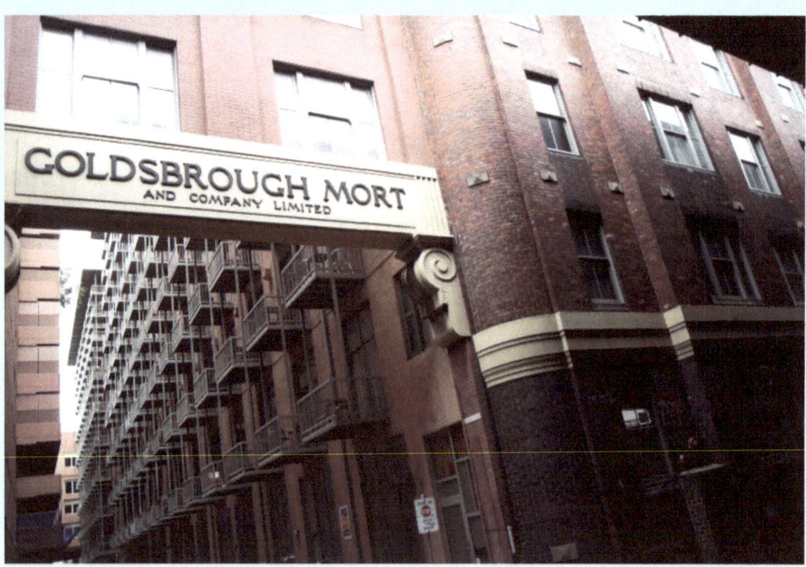

Significant landmarks in Pyrmont

The Goldsbrough is a heritage listed building that is in the heart of one of the historic areas of Sydney.

A brief note about the local development would make one not only appreciate the building itself but also the area in which it is housed.

Pyrmont is a small area but it has a wealth of history which is evident in the architecture of the region.

How to get to landmark locations around the Goldsbrough building on foot

The Goldsbrough building is located at 243 Pyrmont Street, Pyrmont, NSW, 2009.

The main streets close to the building are Allen Street, Harris Street, Pyrmont Bridge Road and Bulwara Road.

Fish Market: Follow Pyrmont Street to the Fire Station building and turn into Gipps Street. Follow Gipps Street and then Pyrmont Bridge Road to the Fish Market.

Edwin Davey Flour Mill: From the Fish Market, cross Pyrmont Bridge Road and follow a walking track to the Wentworth Park Light Rail station. Exit the station, then turn left and walk for about 10 meters to reach the stairs to Jones Street. At the foot of the stairs look into the bushes you will find the Weigh Bridge for the Edwin Davey Flour Mill.

Alternatively from Harris Street turn into Upper Fig Street. At the intersection of Bulwara Road locate Fig Street. Follow Fig Street until you reach Jones Street. Turn right into Jones Street and walk about 100 meters.

At the end of Jones Street, there are stairs (and a lift) to lead you to the lower level ground. At the bottom of the stairs on your right hand side hidden in the bushes is the Weigh Bridge for the Edwin Davey Flour Mill.

Darling Harbour and the International Convention Centre Sydney (ICC Sydney): From level two of the Goldsbrough building, use the walk way to cross Pyrmont Street. Follow the walking signs through the car park until you reach a lift (or stairs).

At the ground floor, follow the signs to outside of the car park, you will see the Convention Centre Light Train Station.

The ICC Sydney and Darling Harbour are on the other side of the Darling Drive.

Pyrmont Bridge: From the ICC Sydney and Darling Harbour, the Pyrmont Bridge is visible. You can walk to it either along the shore or through the Harbourside Shopping Centre.

Alternatively from the Goldsbrough building follow Pyrmont Street then turn right into Pyrmont Bridge Road, walk towards the intersection, with a view of the city skylines, you will see the Pyrmont Bridge.

Groceries: At the corner of Allen Street and Harris Street there are stores selling fruits, vegetables and food. There are many shops on Harris Street, Pyrmont Bridge Road and inside the Harbourside shopping centre.

Lord Wolseley Hotel and Quarry Green: From Harris Street turn to Upper Fig Street and then turn left into the Bulwara Road. The Wolseley Hotel is at 265 Bulwara Rd, Ultimo NSW 2007. Quarry Green is the park in front of the hotel.

Harris Street.

Harris Street contains numerous historic buildings where people in the last century lived and worked.

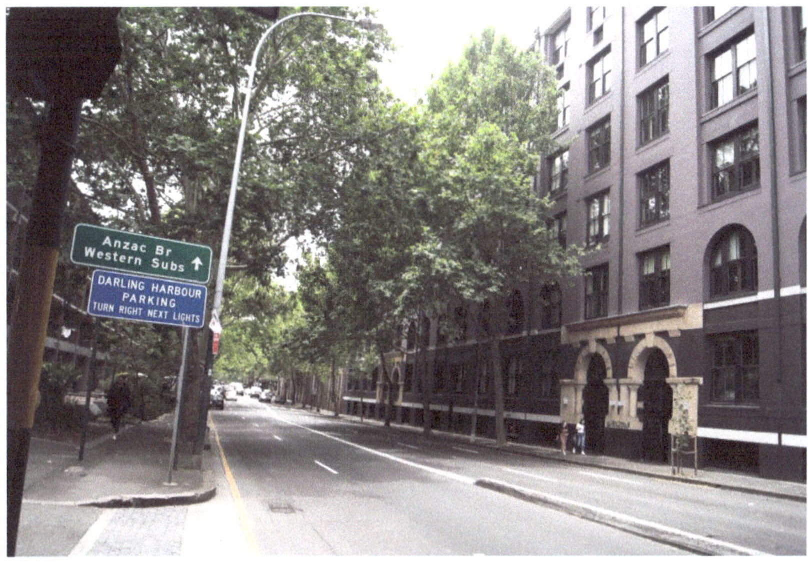

Shops and hotels along Harris Street.

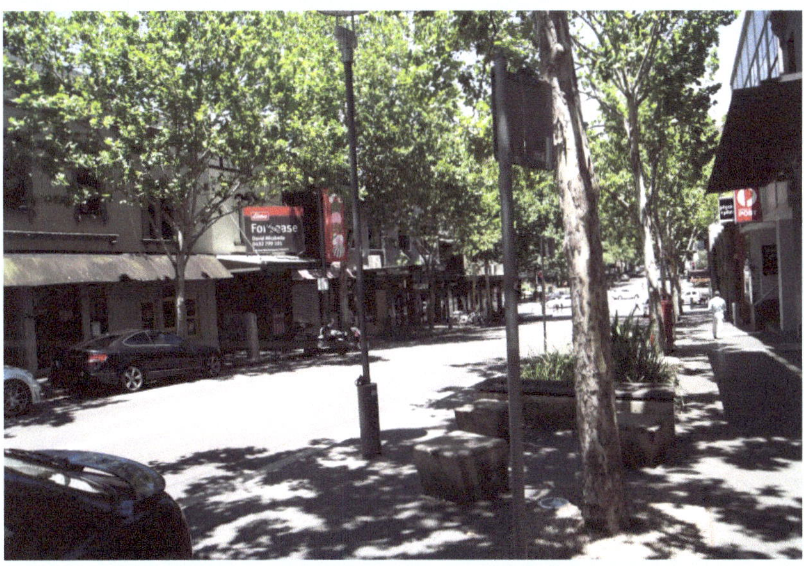

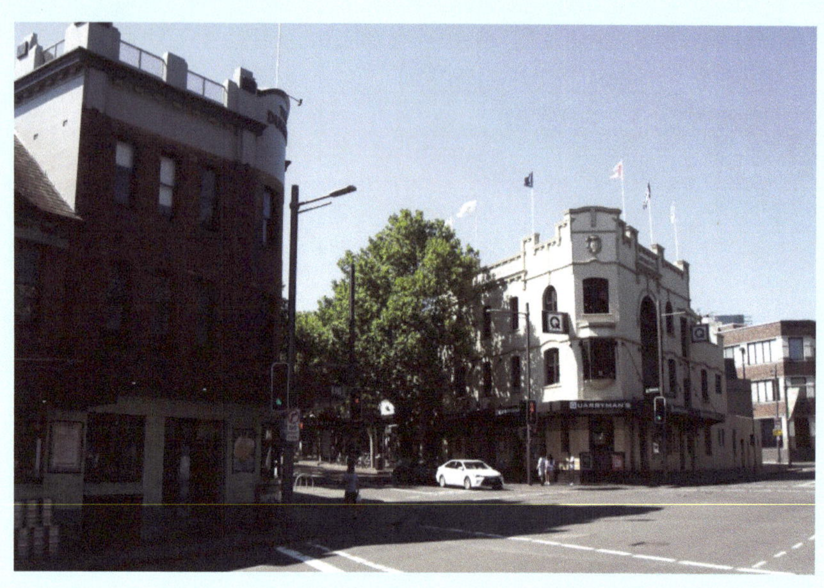

Corner of Harris Street and Pyrmont Bridge Road

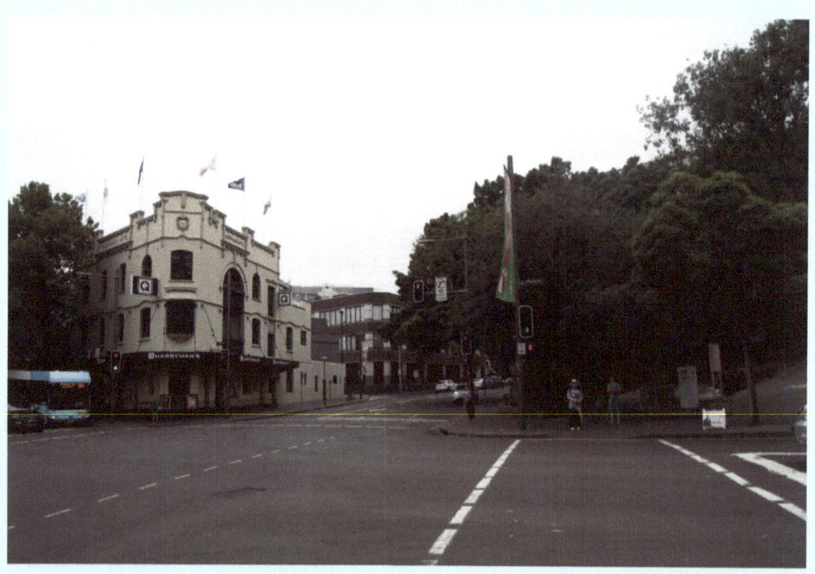

From Gipps Street looking towards the Fish Market

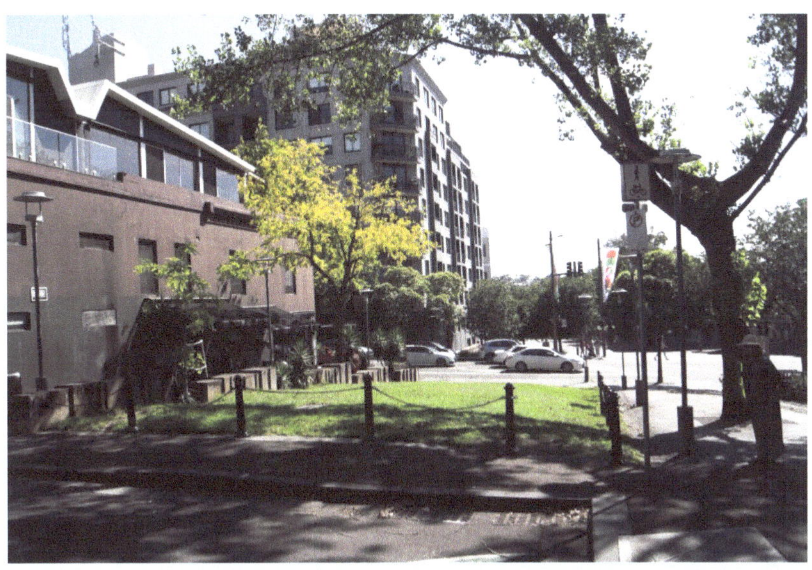

Fish Market Entrance

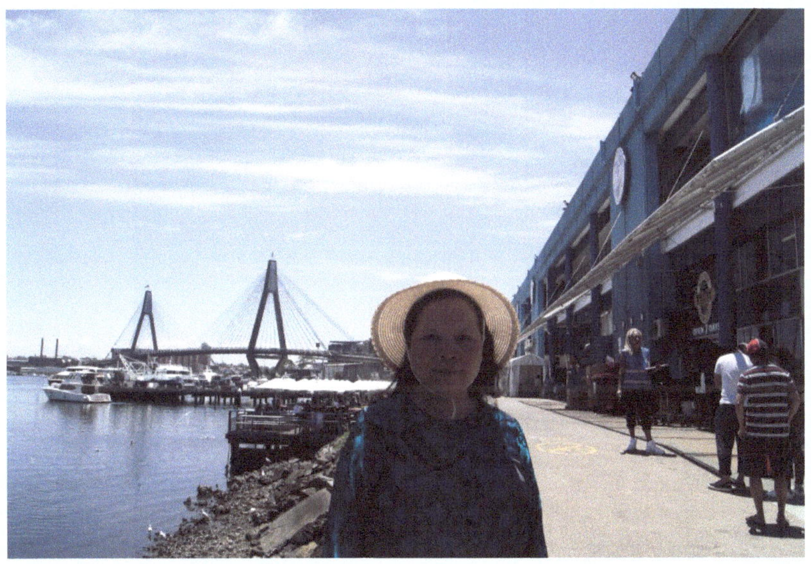

The Hordern Fountain: at the corner of Pyrmont Street and Pyrmont Bridge Road an almost unnoticeable fountain is a reminder of a bygone era (1896). It was built by the sculptor W P McIntosh from local Pyrmont sandstones. The plinth demonstrates fine carving with classical detailing.

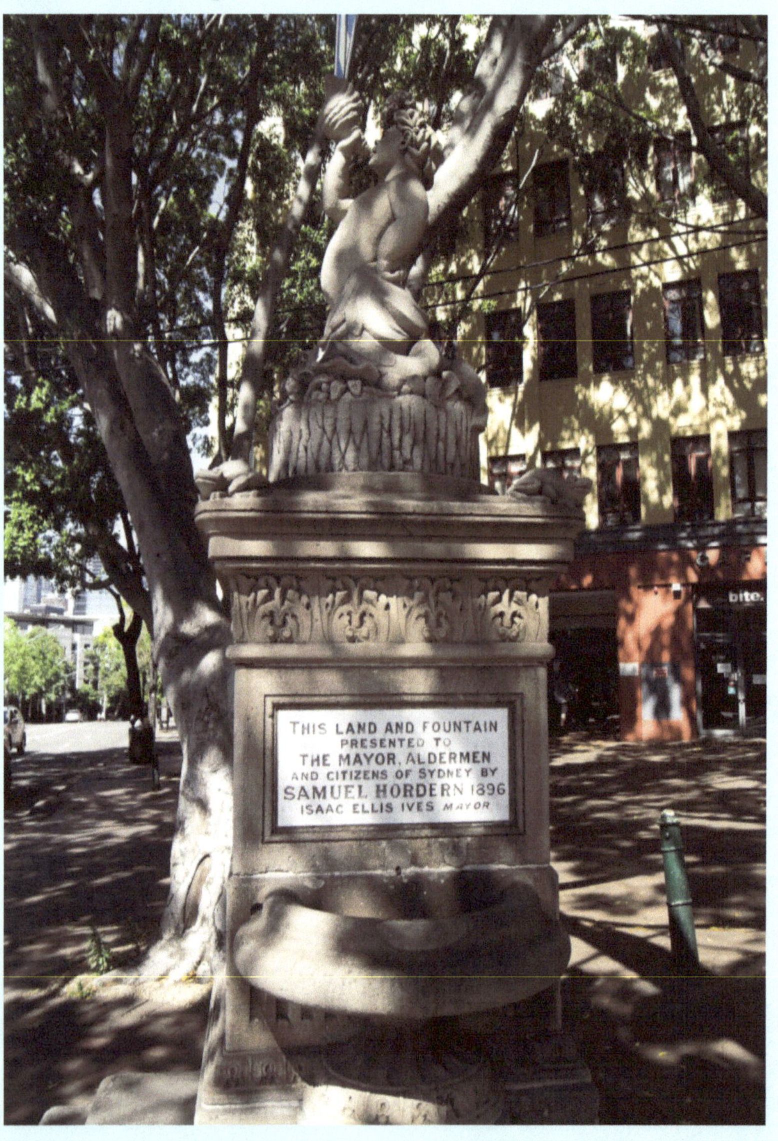

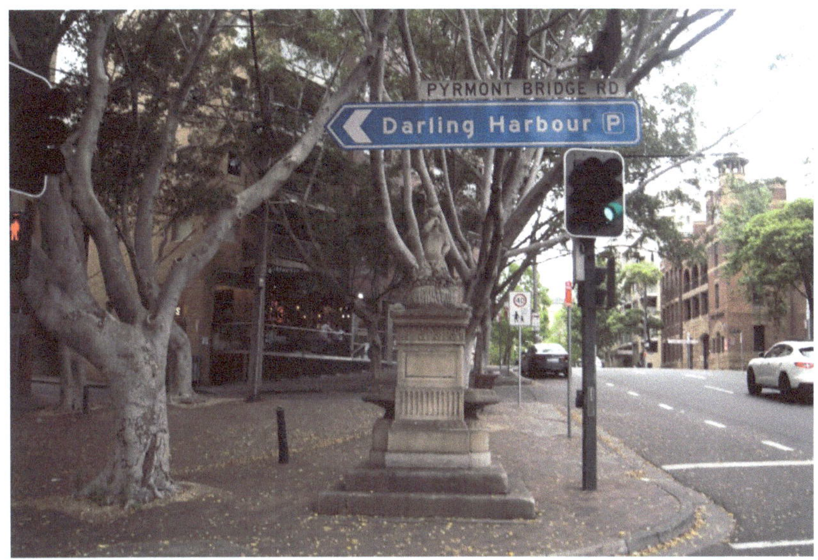

John Taylor Wool Store: was built in 1893, Federation Warehouse architectural style with recessed arches.

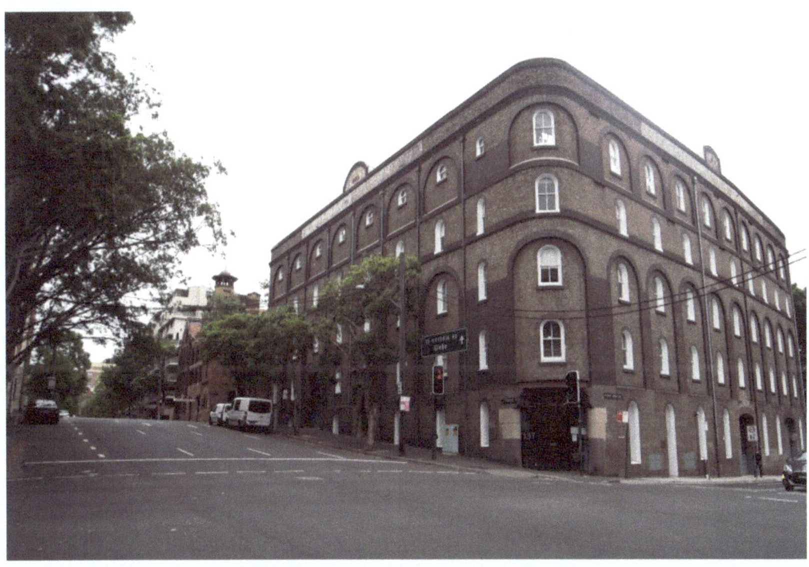

To Pyrmont Bridge via Pyrmont Bridge road

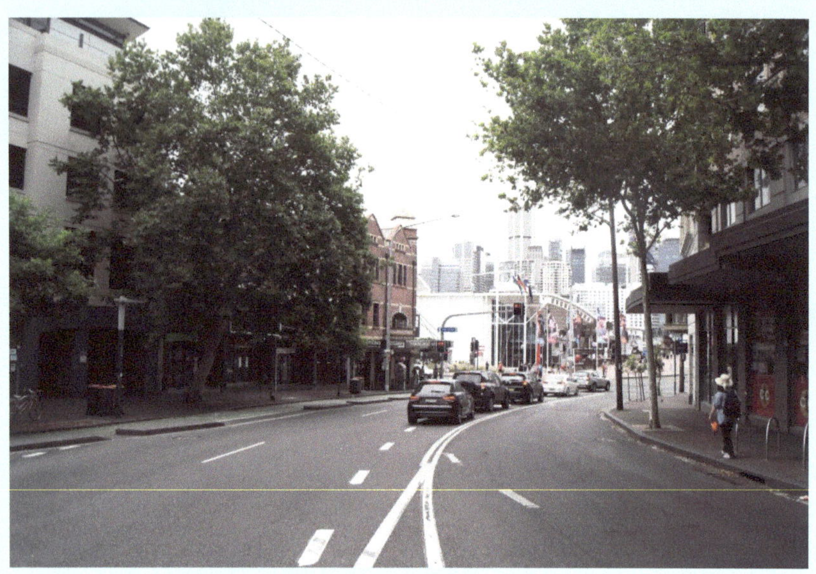

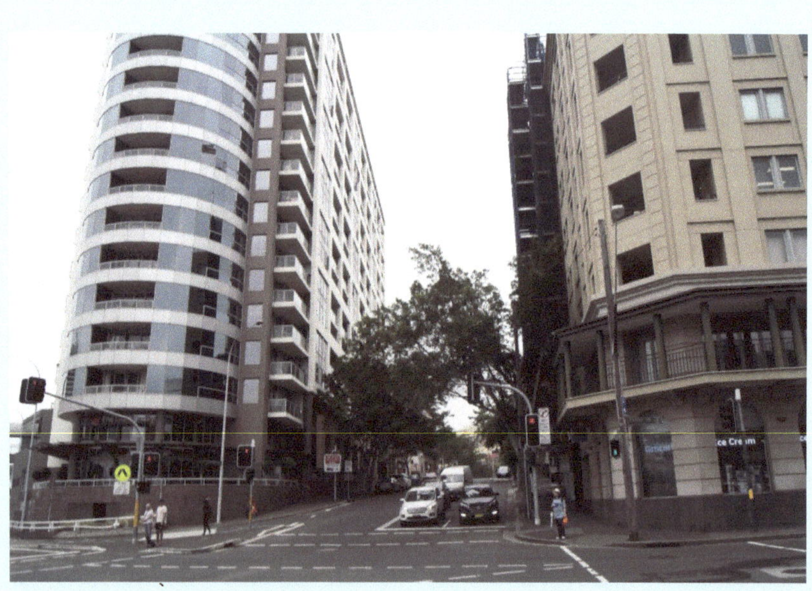

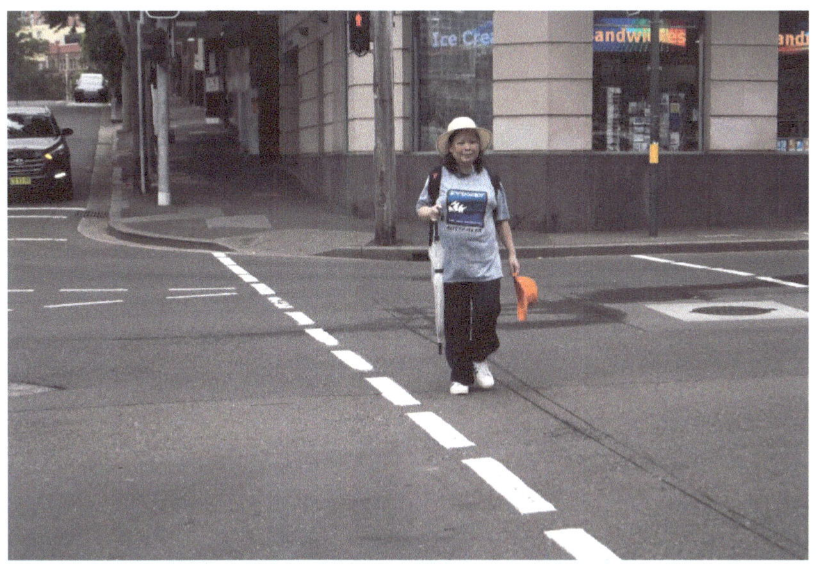

Pyrmont Bridge Road Hotel, built in 1914, retains original features such as the belvedere tower and art nouveau tiles.

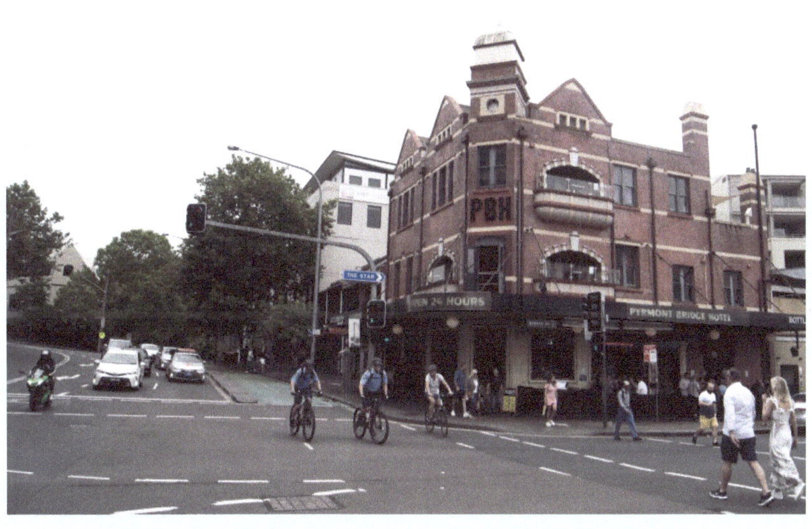

Quarries

During the turn of the century, Pyrmont quarries supplied sandstones for building numerous structures around Sydney and regional areas as well as overseas.

Pergatory Quarry was built as a wool store.

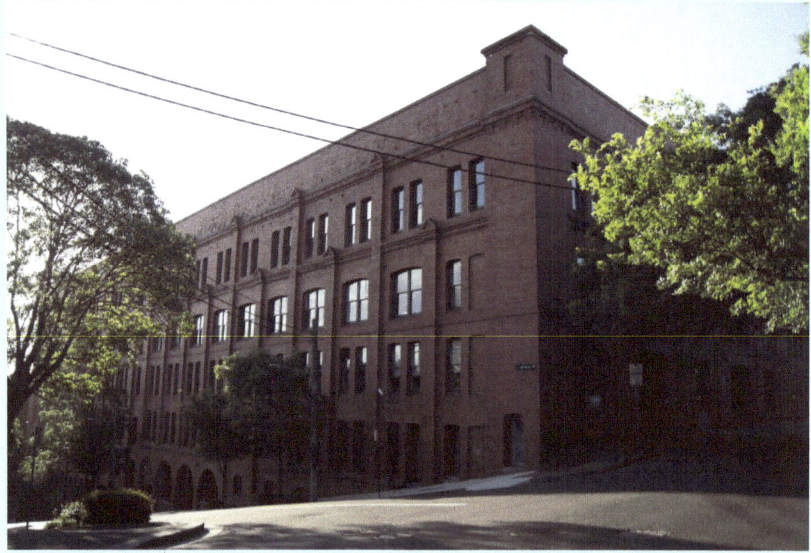

Quarry Lane and the historic houses nearby the quarry.

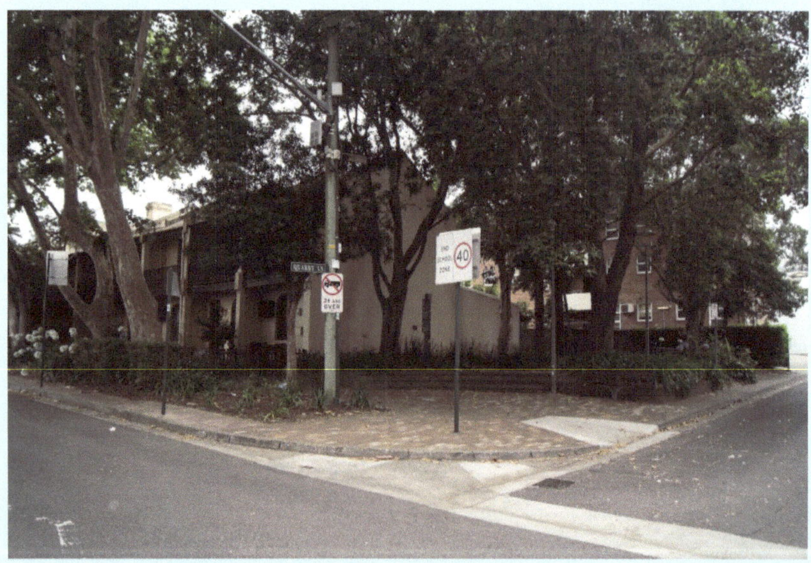

Port and Railways

During a large part of the last century Darling Harbour was a major port. A glance at the map of the region shows that one side of Pyrmont and Murray streets were storages and offices associated with the port activities and other side was railway tracks and industrial sheds where all the porting activities took place.

The steam trains were shunting back and forth all the way from the Central railway station to both sides of Darling Harbour moving cargos of wool, grains, stones and various industrial and agricultural goods. The foot paths underneath the Pyrmont Bridge housed rail tracks.

The railway from Darling Harbour to Wardell Road Junction (Railway junction alongside Dulwich Hill Railway station) connecting Darling Harbour to the rural areas of NSW was built by deep cutting into the stones and building tunnels and viaducts.

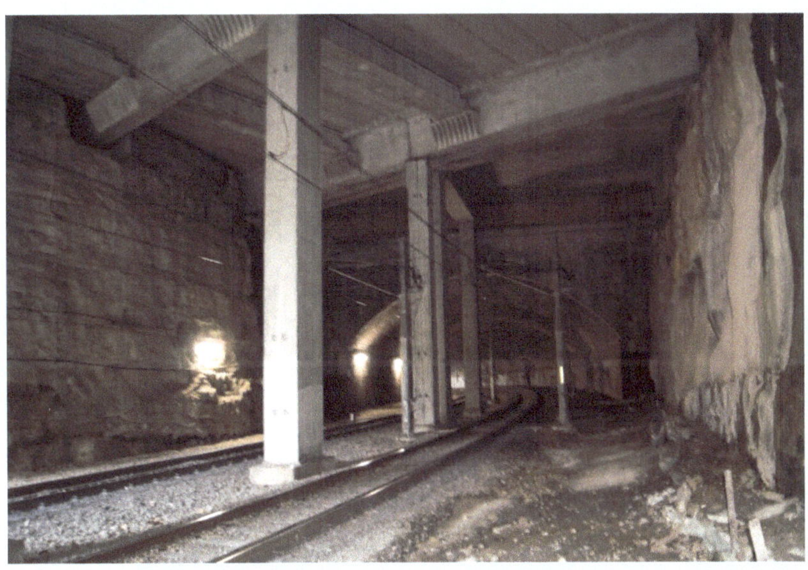

From John Street Square station the cuttings deep into the stones is visible and the brickworks are examples of the workmanships of the period.

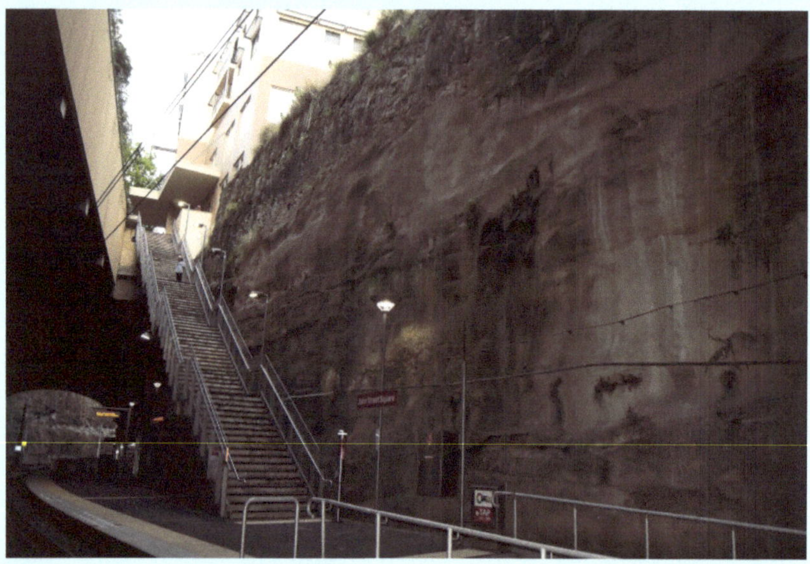

Now only light rail passes through the cuttings and tunnels.

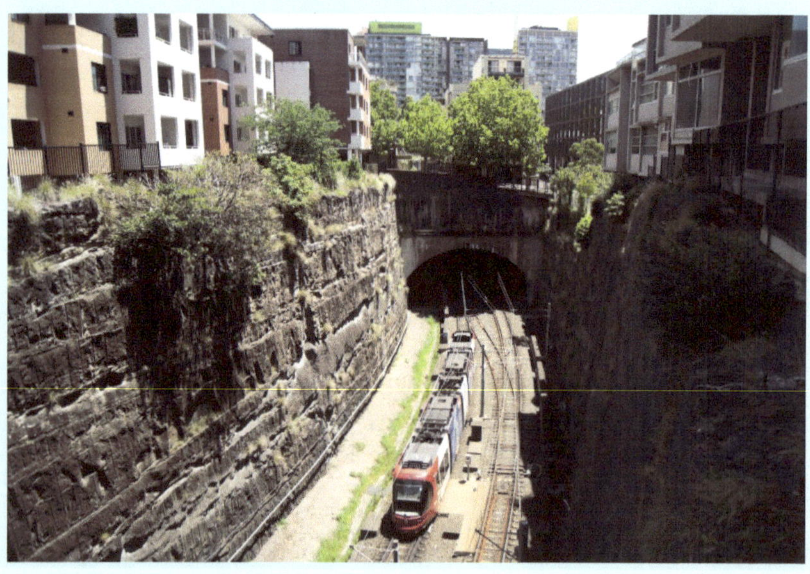

Wentworth Park: Viaduct across Wentworth Park.

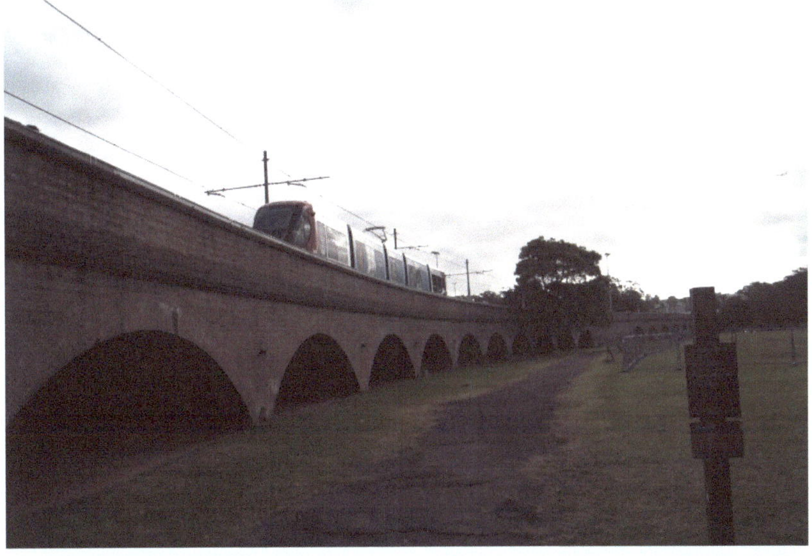

The Edwin Davey Flour Mill was built in 1896 and is located at the end of Jones street, near Wentworth Park light rail station.

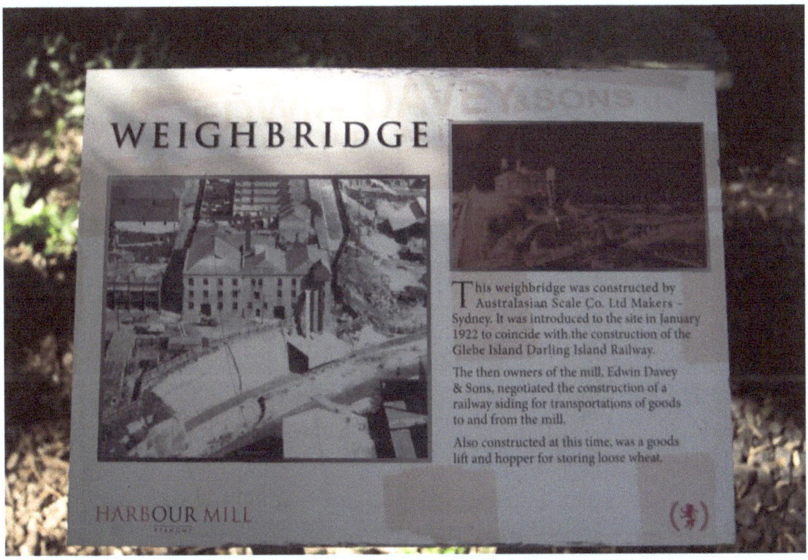

The grain was delivered to the Edwin Davey Flour Mill and processed flour was carried away by rail. The photos show the weighbridge and façade of the building.

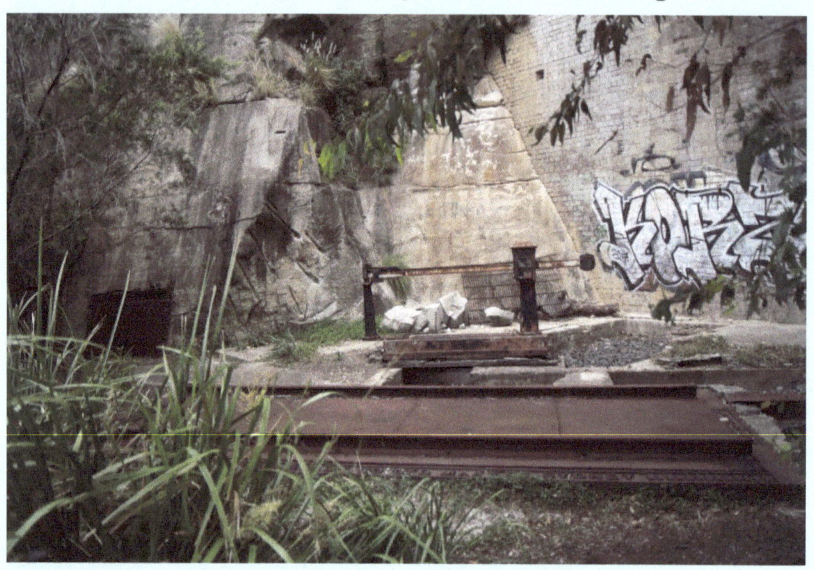

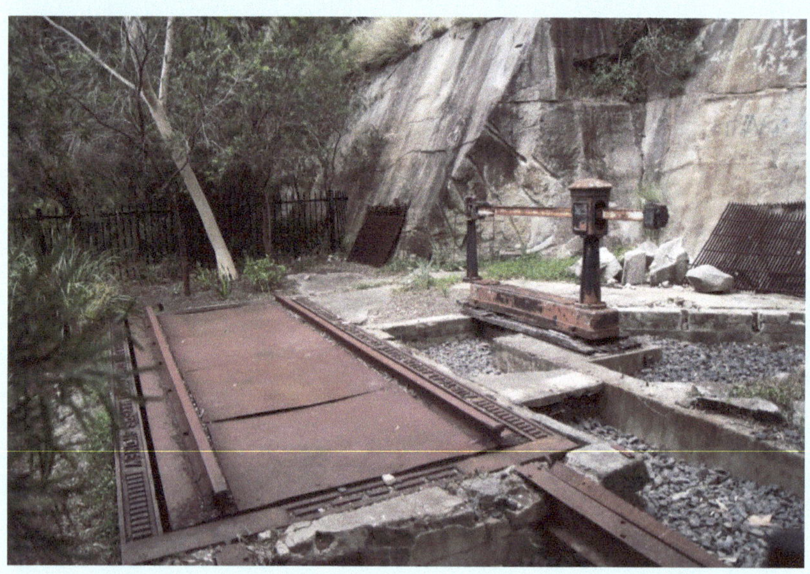

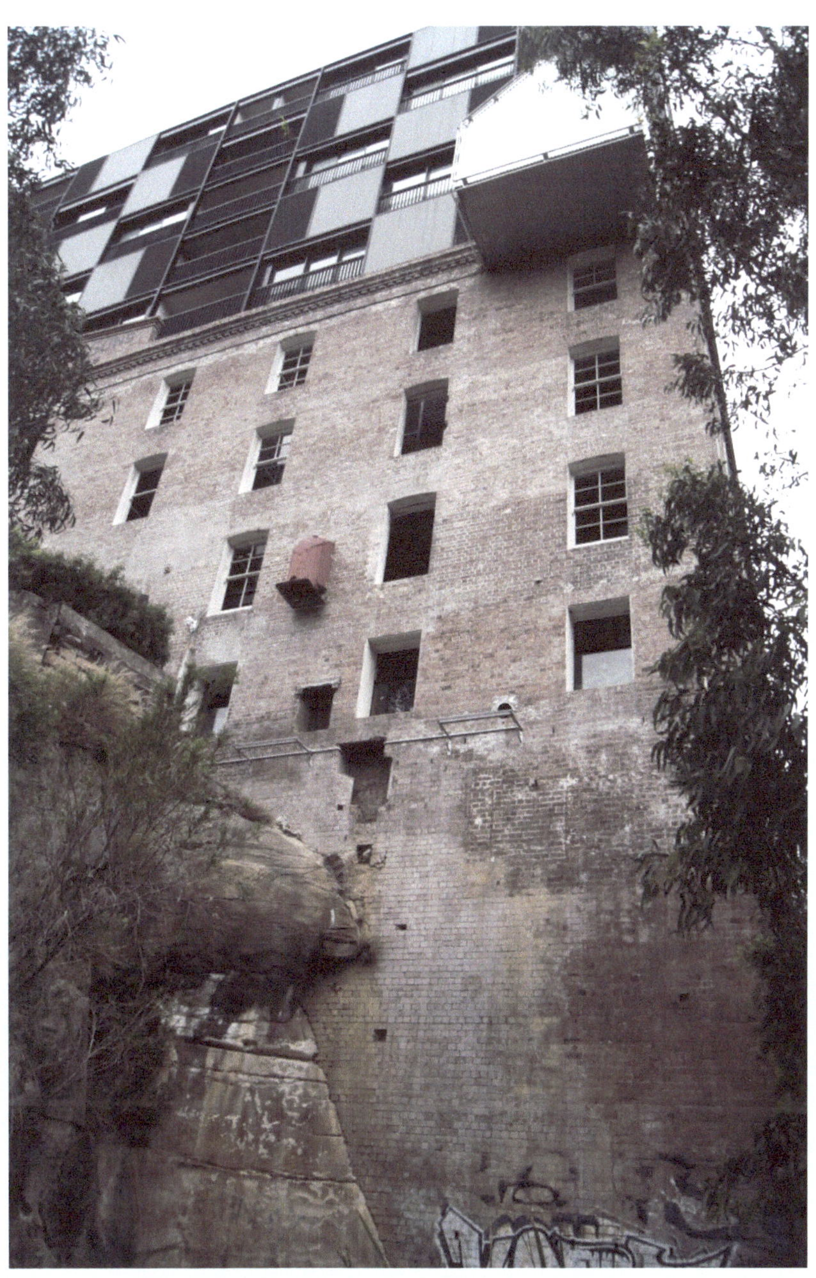

The Electric Power Station, at 42 Pyrmont Street, was built in 1904 and decommissioned in 1993.

The huge carving on the sandstones shows "Municipal Council of Sydney". Above it in black lettering: "Sydney Electric 1904 Lighting Station".

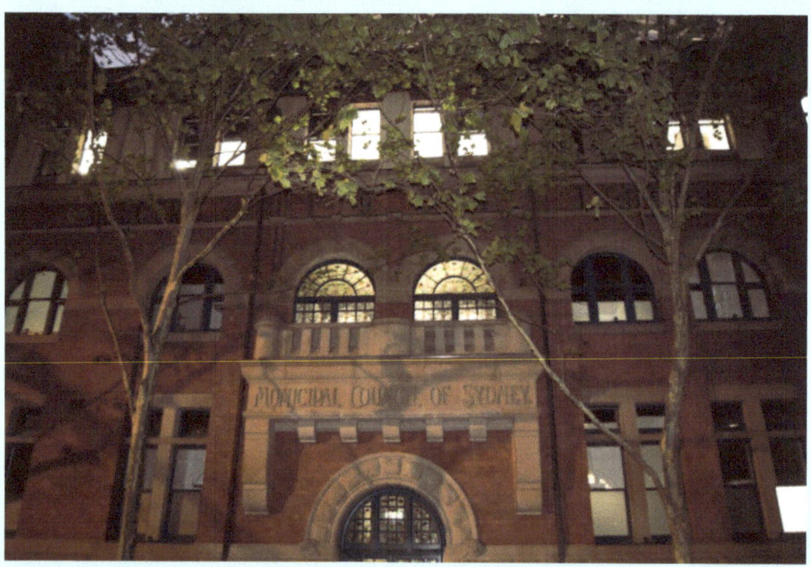

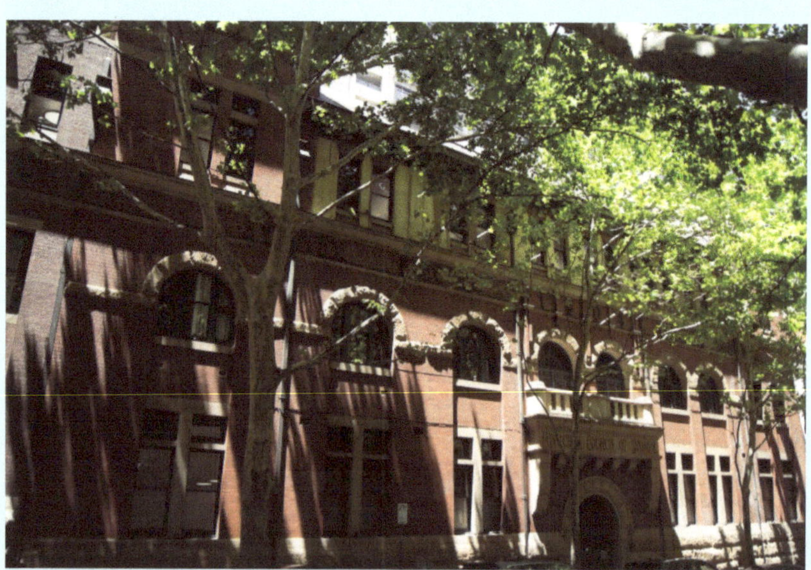

The Fire Station was built in 1906, in Federation Free Style. Its numerous features are a feast for the eyes. While enjoying the site, please take care as the building is still used for its original purpose.

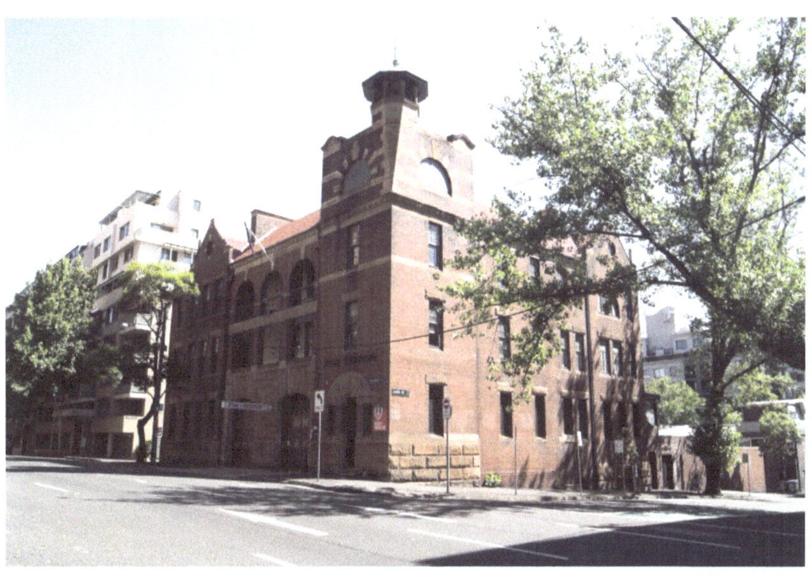

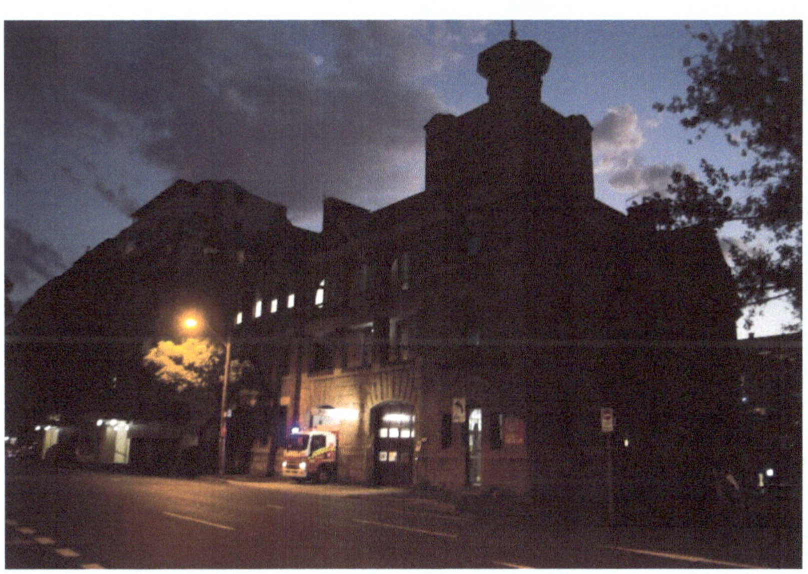

The former Pyrmont Public School, a Victorian Italianate style building with a 3-storey centrally placed bell tower, was constructed in 1892.

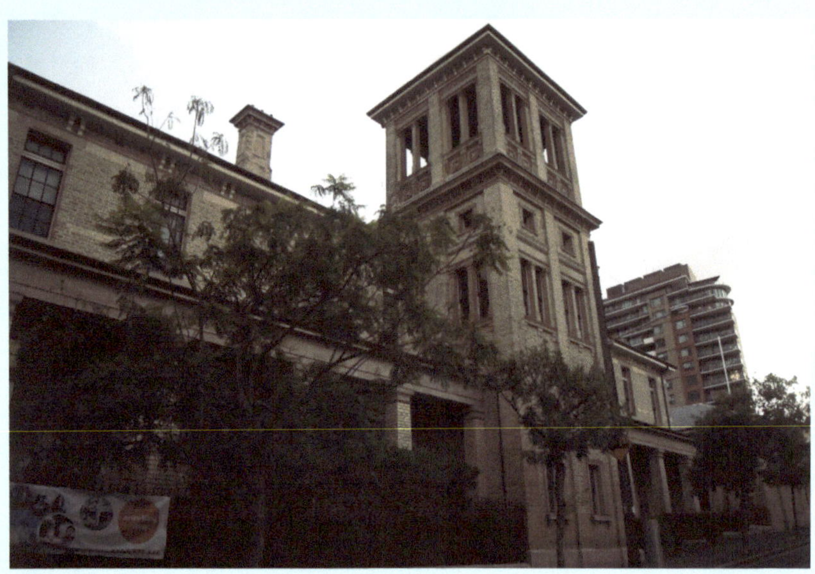

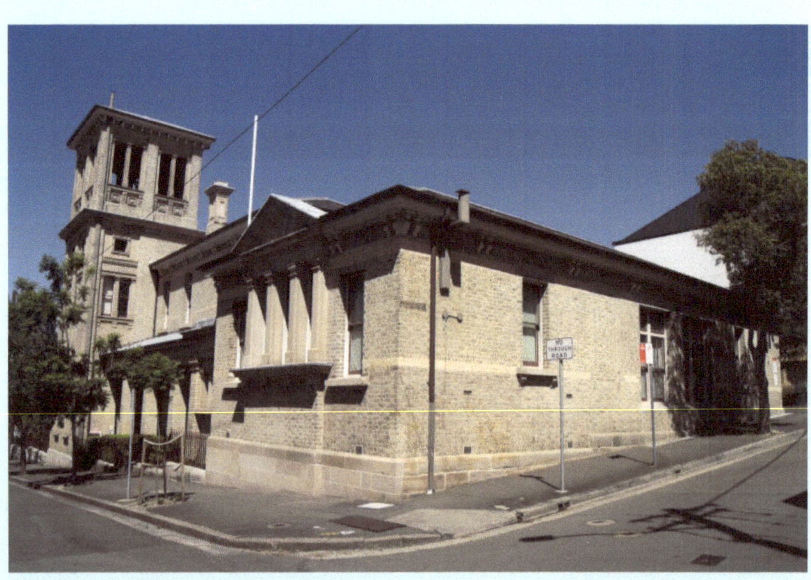

Residential Areas and Local Food

Within walking distance from the Goldsbrough building there are stone houses, local eateries, parks and schools, catered for the locals as well as visitors.

Lord Wolseley Hotel and Quarry Green

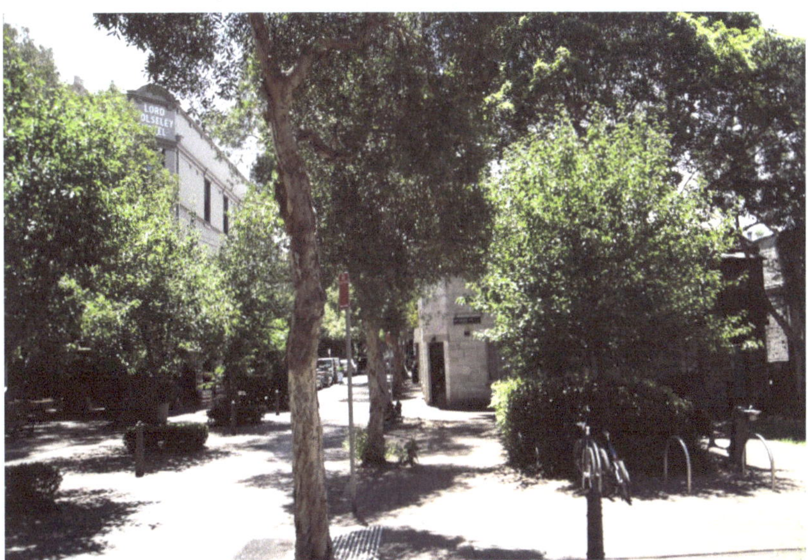

Terminus Hotel on Harris Street

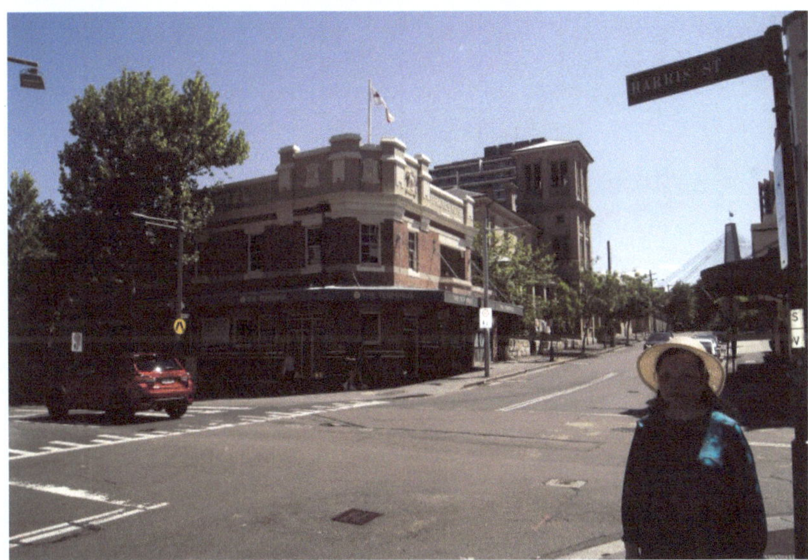

The Angel of Peace was unveiled on 8 April 1922. Pyrmont War Memorial is surmounted by an angel of peace carrying a shield in honour of the men of Pyrmont and Ultimo who served during the Great War 1914-1919.

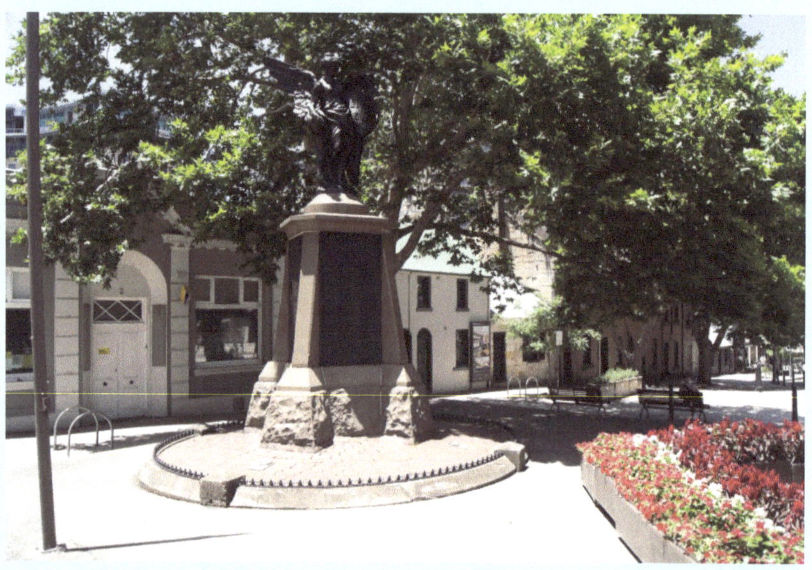

Pyrmont Post Office, for over 100 years, was built in 1901 Federation Free Style using surplus sandstones.

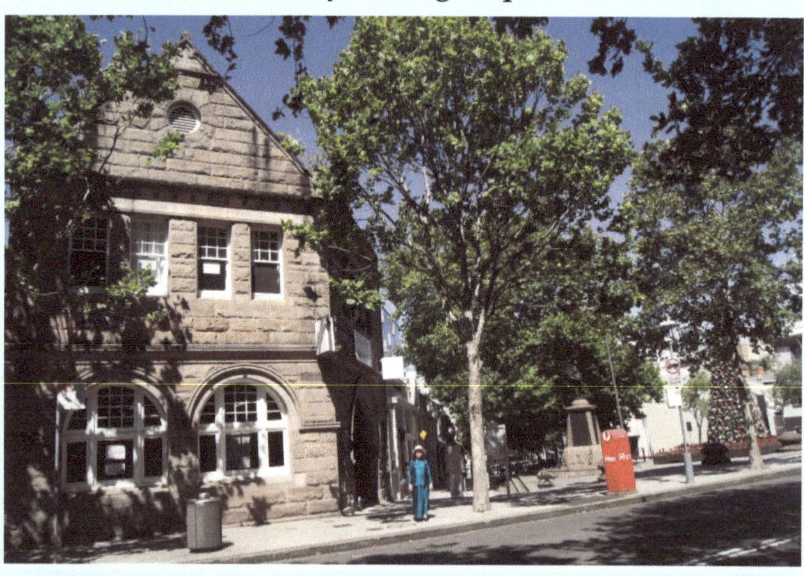

Giba Park and Pirrama Park

Visitors and locals can enjoy the views of both Sydney Bridge and Anzac Bridge from the same beautiful park.

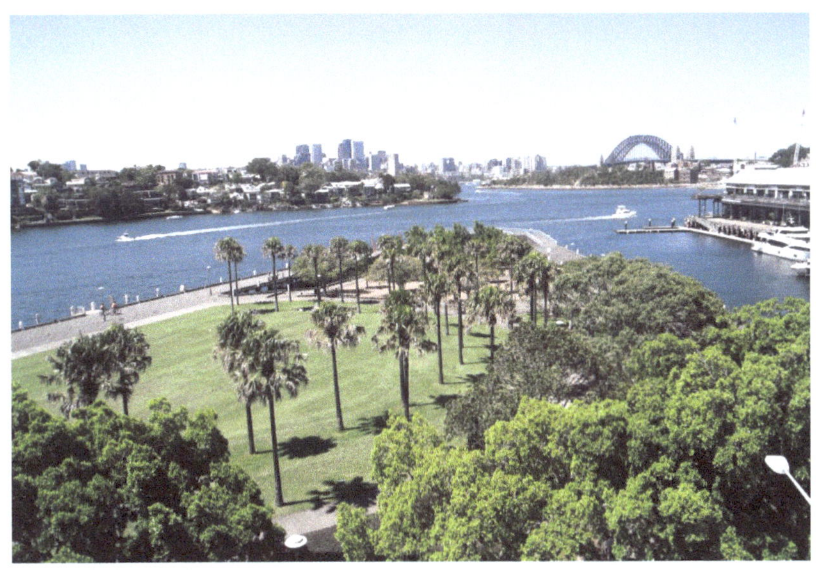

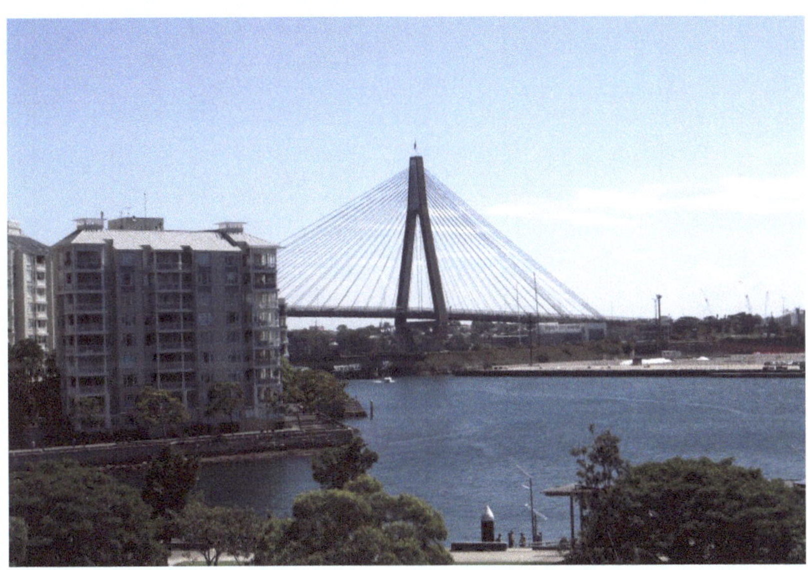

'Nothing is softer or more flexible than water,
yet nothing can resist it.'
Lao Tzu.

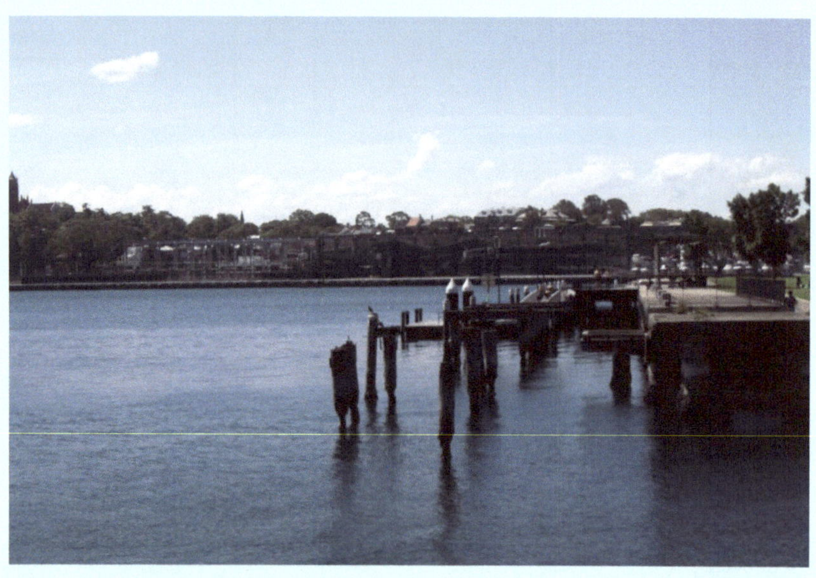

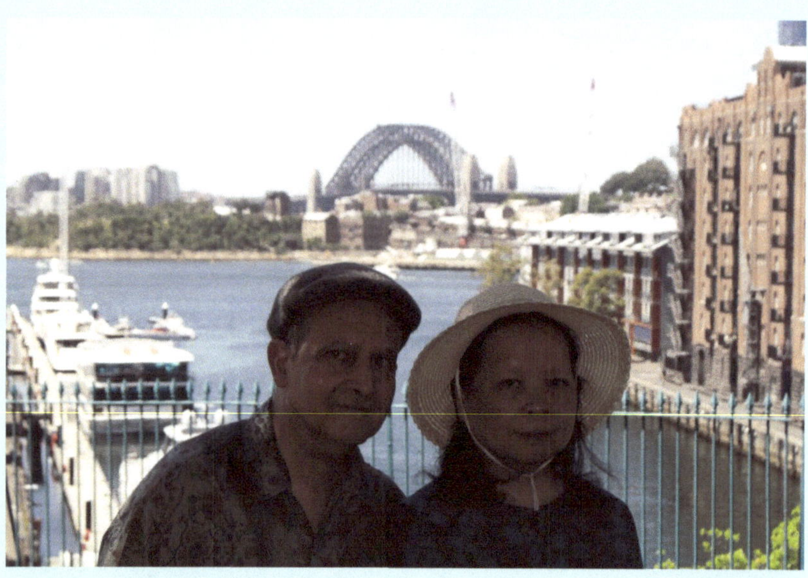

Bahá'u'lláh (November 1817 - May 1892) is a prophet, the founder of the Baha'i Faith.

Abdu'l-Bahá (May 1844 – November 1921) was the Bahá'í Faith's leading exponent, renowned as a champion of social justice and an ambassador for international peace.

Buddha (5th to 4th century BC) is a prophet, the founder of Buddhism.

Confucius (51 – 479 BC) was a Chinese philosopher and politician of the Spring and Autumn period who was traditionally considered the paragon of Chinese sages.

Ralph Waldo Emerson (1803 – 1882) known by Waldo, was an American essayist, lecturer, philosopher, and poet who led the transcendentalist movement of the mid-19th century

Gustave Flaubert (December 1821 – May 1880) was a French novelist. He has been considered the leading exponent of literary realism in his country.

Henry Ford (July 1863 – April 1947) was an American industrialist and business magnate, founder of the Ford Motor Company, and chief developer of the assembly line technique of mass production.

Thomas Jefferson (April 1743 – July 1826) was an American statesman, diplomat, lawyer, architect, philosopher, and Founding Father who served as the third president of the United States from 1801 to 1809.

Dalai Lama is the head monk of Tibetan Buddhism. The current one is the 14th Dalai Lama who was born in July 1935.

Antonio Machado (July 1875 – February 1939) was a Spanish poet and one of the leading figures of the Spanish literary movement known as the Generation of '98.

Psalms: The Book of Psalms is a book of the Christian Old Testament.

Rumi (September 1207 – December 1273) was a 13th century Persian poet.

William Shakespeare (April 1564 – April 1616) was an English playwright, poet, and actor, widely regarded as the greatest writer in the English language and the world's greatest dramatist.

Socrates (470 – 399 BC) was a classical Greek (Athenian) philosopher. He is the first moral philosopher of the Western ethical tradition of thought and one of the founders of Western philosophy.

Henry David Thoreau (July 1817 – May 1862) was an American naturalist, essayist, poet, and philosopher.

Lao Tzu (6th or 4th century BC) was a Chinese philosopher.

Adeline Virginia Woolf (January 1882 – March 1941) was an English writer, considered one of the more important modernist 20th century authors and also a pioneer in the use of stream of consciousness as a narrative device.

Sir Christopher Wren (October 1632 – March 1723) was one of the most highly acclaimed English architects in history, as well as an anatomist, astronomer, geometer, and mathematician-physicist.

References

www.bahai.org

www.darlingharbour.com

www.dictionaryofsydney.org

www.en.wikipedia.org

www.goldsbrough.com.au

www.heritage.nsw.gov.au

www.minh-hien.com

www.pyrmonthistory.net.au

www.sea.museum

www.visitsydneyaustralia.com.au